Alchemy
of the Heart

Other books and recordings by Michael Brown

*The Presence Process: A Healing Journey
into Present Moment Awareness*

*The Presence Process: A Journey into Present
Moment Awareness*, Revised Edition

A Walk Through The Presence Process (4 CD set)

The Heart Is the Healer (CD)

Our Heart Is Our Responsibility (CD)

The Radiance of Intimacy (CD)

Awakening to Innocence / Inner Sense (3 DVD set)

Alchemy
of the Heart

Transforming Turmoil into Peace
through Emotional Integration

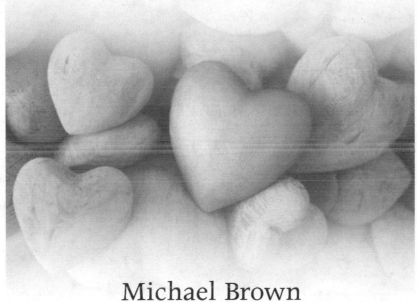

Michael Brown

Namaste Publishing
Vancouver, Canada

Library and Archives Canada Cataloguing in Publication

Brown, Michael, 1962–
  Alchemy of the heart: transforming turmoil into peace through emotional integration /
  Michael Brown.
  ISBN 978-1-897238-37-0
  1. Spiritual life. 2. Consciousness—Religious aspects. 3. Quietude. 4. Self-realization.
  5. Health. 6. Alternative Medicine. 7. Addiction. I. Title.
BD311.K44 2008   204'.4   C2008-902672-9

Published by Namaste Publishing
PO Box 62084
Vancouver, BC, Canada V6J 4A3
www.namastepublishing.com

Distributed by PGW, Berkeley, CA USA
Cover design by Gabreyhl Zintoll
Interior book design by Val Speidel
Printed and bound in Canada by Friesens Corporation

dedicated to

Trevor George Tinker
For being a father to me.
You are often in my thoughts,
Always in my heart.
Thank you.

Alchemy of the Heart

How do we become alchemists of the heart?

The quality of our experiences is a reflection of the condition of our inner being. For our experiences to change, we must make adjustments at the causal point of these experiences. The causal point of all that occurs in our lives is the heart.

To be an alchemist of the heart is to impact the quality of our external experiences by making internal adjustments.

The key to the heart's alchemical magic is to accept responsibility for the quality of our experiences. When we accept responsibility, we begin to turn the base metal of our unintegrated emotions into the gold of harmonious living. We then realize the peace we seek in the world.

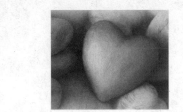

Contents

Acknowledgements

CONSTANCE KELLOUGH—for a beautiful and tender vision that makes so much possible for so many. Thank you, thank you, thank you. Dr. Paul Bahder—for the landing and takeoff strip, the creation of The Presence Portal, and our wonderful friendship. Kathy Cholod— for spreading the word, directing traffic, endless enthusiasm, putting up with this moody Leo, and having the patience of a saint! How would we do this without you? Elizabeth McManus—for the lattes, spontaneous laughter, keeping it real, things & stuff, and everything unsaid that flows in between. Teresa Bahder for believing so sincerely in The Presence Process and staying true to the heart of "the work." Nora Morin—for the behind-the-scenes work in the engine room that places an expression on the face of this work. Diane and Ludovico Iezzo—for picking me up, dropping me off, and all the fun and food along the way. David Robert Ord—for sharing your wisdom, insight, and guidance, and for saturating this text with your masterful editorial touch —thank you. For all gardeners of the heart—may our harvest be authentic, have integrity, and lead us into an ever-deepening, intimate encounter with our humanity.

Note to the Reader

THROUGHOUT *this book, I use a play on words to help us see things in a different light and understand them at a deeper level. I use the vocabulary of the mind to help us impact ourselves at an emotional level. Hence, for the word realize, I use real eyes. To do so causes us to consider what we are doing when we "realize" something. We are seeing with real eyes—looking at something in an authentic way. Presenting certain words in this way is a perceptual tool used to create an opening of awareness within the reader.*

Introduction

AFTER writing *The Presence Process,* my journey transformed from personally facilitating individuals through this procedure to sharing this work within the context of group encounters. Out of this evolved a way of presenting this work that clearly communicates the role of the heart within our quest for authenticity, integrity, and intimacy.

Because I cannot personally deliver this presentation to everyone who is drawn to this work, and because I *real eyes* the significance of the perceptual insight and integration it invites, I have chosen to make it accessible through *Alchemy Of The Heart*.

Like *The Presence Process,* this book is a deliberately designed perceptual journey. It empowers us to transform the quality of our human experience by revealing the alchemical role of our heart. The perceptual journey it initiates inspires a movement of our awareness from revolutionary to effortless evolutionary behavior.

By continuing to behave as if we can authentically transform our circumstances through imposing our will upon the outside world, we constantly enter revolutionary behavior. The very word "revolutionary" reveals the outcome—we inevitably *revolve* into similar circumstances from which we are attempting to extricate ourselves, and often worse.

A revolutionary approach is born of a mentality that seeks to liberate itself with the same approach that it perceives to be the cause of its suppression. By resorting to this reactive mentality, a revolutionary always becomes an oppressor. This in turn seeds a whole new crop of revolutionaries.

Alchemy Of The Heart invites us to consider the option of evolutionary behavior, an approach to adjusting the quality of our human experience that doesn't lead us back into the experiential circumstances from which we seek liberation, but takes us beyond.

Evolutionary behavior transforms an experience by using a means completely different from whatever is perceived as the method of oppression. To become evolutionary is to *real eyes oneself as the only oppressor to be dethroned.*

By embracing an inwardly-directed approach to adjusting outer experiences, evolutionary individuals navigate their experience according to a completely new paradigm. To communicate the perceptual shift that makes evolutionary behavior possible is at the heart of this book.

In keeping with the resonance of non-interference, *Alchemy of the Heart* does not ask us to step upon any new path or alter our allegiance to the one we are currently treading. Instead, it empowers us to use every fiber of our accumulated life experience as a means of integrating our current circumstances in a manner that reveals a clear point of continuation.

Unlike *The Presence Process*, *Alchemy of the Heart* requires no systematic procedure, other than reading, to reap the benefits of the fruits within the text. It is intended to effortlessly inspire, challenge, trigger, and question our human experience in a manner inviting verification, not through debate or discussion, but through consciously transforming the way we perceive the purpose of our presence upon Earth, and then encouraging us to engage the wondrous play of life accordingly.

Real Eyes

THE stranger sat quietly amid the ever-shifting tide of the morning market, quiet enough to be noticed by a young boy whose heart was at peace.

"Hello," greeted the young boy.

"Good morning," the stranger said, smiling kindly.

"Where are you from?" asked the boy, sitting down next to the stranger.

"What makes you think I am from somewhere else?" inquired the stranger with a glint in his eyes.

"There is a different light that shines from you," replied the boy.

"You can see this light?" asked the stranger, curious.

"Not with my eyes," the boy explained softly, as if sharing a secret, "but I feel it."

"Ah," said the stranger, also softening his voice, "you see it with your heart."

"Yes," said the boy. They sat in silence together for what felt like eternity. Then the boy reached out and placed his hand gently on the stranger's forearm. "Can you take me there?"

"No," said the stranger, "but as I sit here and quietly enjoy this beautiful morning, I am pointing the way. And anyway," he chuckled, placing his arm around the boy's shoulder, "we cannot be taken to somewhere we already are."

Authenticity

IMAGINE our life experience unfolding within a restaurant.

When we begin awakening to the possibility that there may be more to our life than the mundane assumption that we are here merely to earn a living, we are like dissatisfied customers sitting in the restaurant. We do not appreciate the food that is being served because it isn't what we ordered. We do not appreciate the company we are keeping because people, for the most part, annoy us. We spend much of our time moaning about our plight, then complaining to the waiter, even though it is common knowledge the waiter does not cook.

The poor quality of our experience may cause us to ask an important question: "Why does this keep happening to me?"

When we examine our life experience and sincerely ask "Why?" we initiate a quest for *authenticity*.

The meaning of authenticity is revealed through the phonetics of the word. *Authentic* phonetically contains the word *author*. By asking "Why?" we are really asking "Who is the *author* of the experience I am having?"

This inquiry awakens us to the presence of the physical, mental, and emotional mechanisms that manufacture our human experience. Bringing awareness to these mechanisms empowers us to become the author of our encounter with life.

The culmination of our quest for authenticity is an awakening into an awareness of *what we are* as opposed to *who we think we are supposed to be.*

Integrity

WE enter the next phase of our journey when we leave our seat in the restaurant and discover the kitchen. This is an exciting, heady, and sensual part of the experience.

When we step into the kitchen, we real eyes we are able to cook our own meals, and that there are all sorts of ingredients, utensils, and appliances with which to interact.

This is the part of the journey when we enthusiastically engage in spiritual practices like yoga and meditation, explore tools like crystals and tarot cards, and immerse ourselves in energetic procedures like affirmative processes and emotional cleansing.

This phase of the journey is seductive. Because we learn so much so quickly, we feel as if we are accomplishing great things.

This experience of being in the kitchen is also enticing because we find the prospect of becoming master chefs entrancing. Consequently, we invariably become stuck in the kitchen for a long, long, long time.

Fortunately, being in the kitchen cooking the food is also the phase of our inner journey that initiates a quest for *integrity*, and it is our acquiring of integrity that eventually frees us from confinement in what may easily become a cul-de-sac.

The term integrity, within the context of this inner journey, refers to the soundness of the structure of our human experience. If a building does not have integrity, a deviation from regular weather patterns may cause it to collapse. The soundness of a building's integrity is dependent upon using the appropriate building materials for the appropriate applications.

We approach integrity authentically within the kitchen experience by gaining a working awareness of which ingredients, utensils, and appliances are used to cook specific delicacies. In terms of our moment-to-moment human experience, we learn the precise function of the physical, mental, and emotional components that go into the manufacture of this experience.

The culmination of our quest for integrity is in *radiating our heart's waking vision* as opposed to *trying to fulfill a dream someone else has for us.*

Intimacy

A FURTHER phase of our inner journey commences when it dawns within our heart that cooked food must disappear completely into good conversation and required nutrition for it to fulfill its purpose.

In other words, there is more to life than living in the kitchen. If we do not come to this realization, we inevitably overcook the food or let it sit out and spoil.

It is through this realization that we eventually leave the kitchen and return to the same seat within the restaurant in which we were sitting when we began inquiring about the source of our discomfort.

Once we return to our seat, it may appear to others that nothing has changed. Our outer state may appear quite similar to that of the person who asked, "Why does this keep happening to me?"

It is true that we are still immersed in the same human experience we were having before our inner journey commenced. However, we are now responding differently to all our encounters. We sit relaxed, enjoying our meal, talking comfortably with others, and treating the waiter with respect and gratitude. We are saturated with awareness of the magnificence of our humanity. We appreciate the gift of life. All our physical, mental, and emotional experiences now become a means to enter the sweet embrace of *intimacy*.

The meaning of intimacy within the context of this unfolding journey is revealed through the phonetics of the word—*into-me-and-see*. We enter the experience of intimacy when *every encounter we pass through presents itself as a divinely guided opportunity to see deeper within ourselves*.

The culmination of our quest for intimacy is when *we honor our life experience as it is*, instead of *behaving as if it were supposed to be different*.

The Portal

LIKE authenticity and integrity, intimacy is not a destination. It is an experiential portal into a very obvious yet simultaneously deeply concealed reality.

Just as the fullness of the experience called integrity awaits us beyond the quest for authenticity, and just as the fullness of the experience called intimacy awaits us beyond the quest for integrity, so too there is an experience that awaits us beyond the sweet embrace of intimacy.

Intimacy awakens us to what the experience of *life* really is. Yet such a statement is just words printed on a page. The experience that intimacy leads us into cannot be communicated through words or arrived at by means of mental contemplation. This is because the mental body does not have a vocabulary competent enough to communicate the felt-parameters of this experience. The mental body is the attribute we use to conceptually encounter our energetic experiences and to translate our interactions with the physical world into thought form. Its language is thinking, analysis, and understanding. *When it comes to the realm of feeling, the mental body is impotent.*

Throughout this text we shall refer to the experience open to us through the portal of intimacy as *entering a conversation with the unspeakable.*

The Blindness

A STRANGER walking along a street late one night comes across a man on his hands and knees beneath the light of a street lamp. He is obviously seeking something.

"Have you lost something?" the stranger asks the seeker.

"Yes, I have lost an important key."

"May I assist you in your search?"

"Thank you, I appreciate the assistance."

They search together for a moment. The area illuminated by the street lamp is small, so it only takes a few moments to scan it thoroughly.

"Are you sure you lost the key here?" the stranger asks the seeker.

"No, I didn't lose it here. I lost it in my home."

"Then why are you looking for it outside under this street lamp?"

"Because the lighting in my home is not working."

We too are in a predicament in which the lighting is out within our home, and so we conveniently search for what is within us where it cannot be found—outside of ourselves.

We are all seeking the answers to our deepest questions in the same manner. We are searching according to the means of perception we currently have available to us—by examining various material aspects of our physical experience, making mental inquiry through our thoughts, and examining the thoughts of others.

Questions Not Meant to Be Answered

THERE are questions that are not meant to be answered. They are only meant to be asked.

If *we* attempt to answer these types of questions, we invariably do so using the process of thinking, and therefore we only receive answers as mental concepts. If we settle for mental concepts, it means we are satisfied with *information*, not *knowledge*. Information is thought-form that has only a mental component to it. Knowledge, on the other hand, contains an integrated physical, mental, *and* emotional component to it.

When we *do not answer a question mentally*, but instead *choose to sit within the resonance of the question*, the answer unfolds organically within our life as an integrated physical, mental, and emotional experience.

This approach to asking questions may not be appropriate for all questions. But it is a highly efficient tool when it comes to deliberately grounding experiential knowledge of the unspeakable into our daily experience.

The more profound our questions, the more profound the life experience we initiate when we do not answer them with mental concepts. Knowing how to ask questions without answering them is the art of initiating revelation.

We may ask, "What is an important question to ask?" Asking a question like this, without answering it mentally, opens the parameters of our personal experience to the horizon of unlimited possibility.

Three Questions

THERE are three questions that, when asked authentically, restore awareness within us of a reality that has become hidden.

Within this text we call this reality "the unspeakable." It is deliberately called the unspeakable to communicate that it cannot be grasped through a purely mental approach. Once an awareness of this reality is restored within us, its vibration radiates into all aspects of our life experience.

The three questions are:

WHAT AM I?

Not who. Asking *who* opens us to personality-driven answers. *Who* has to do with concepts and behavioral traits, not with awareness of our authentic essence.

WHAT IS GOD FOR US?

Again, it is best not to use the word *who*. When God is a *who,* we are invariably dabbling in culturally based belief systems.

WHERE AM I NOW?

This is a question we seldom ask because we assume we know where we are, just as we tend to mistakenly assume we are the conceptual and behavioral personality we have manufactured—the outer identity everyone in our life interacts with. We also tend to mistakenly assume God is the personality-driven identity our religions have fed us, an identity manufactured from within the limitations of our human intellect. In a similar way, we may mistakenly assume *where we are right now* is defined by the physical address or geographical location of our living circumstances. But is it really?

The reason we may struggle to answer these three questions is that we automatically attempt to supply either a physical or mental answer. Yet, neither the physical nor mental aspects of our human experience have the capacity to engage any question whose answer is only available as *a vibrational transmission.*

Therefore, unless we reactivate our capacity to interact directly with our vibrational essence, we remain blind to these answers even when they are closer to us than the air we breathe.

Only through consciously shedding our blindness do we initiate the journey of awakening, leading us from living unconsciously toward a conscious conversation with the unspeakable.

⟨ 2 ⟩

The Pathway of Awareness

OUR awareness travels along an intentional energetic pathway to enter our experience of life upon earth. Its existence is right in front of our nose, yet it remains hidden until shown to us. Throughout this book we call this The Pathway of Awareness.

Once we real eyes how this energetic pathway is in full view of us at all times—yet completely hidden from our awareness until our attention is brought to it—we may wonder what else about our human experience is hidden within plain sight.

This energetic Pathway of Awareness is most clearly visible in the initial development of a newborn child. First, the child is an emotional being; it can only emote. Then, as it learns to use its emotions to communicate, it gradually enters mental awareness. Next, it becomes conscious enough to reach out and deliberately grab hold of and maintain physical contact with something.

Even though the child's emotional, mental, and physical attributes develop simultaneously, there is a systematic energetic pathway that the child's awareness intentionally travels along to enter a full encounter with life upon this earth.

The pathway runs from the emotional, to the mental, to the physical.

The Seven-Year Cycle

THE Pathway of Awareness, from emotional to mental to physical, that we traveled along and continue to travel along in order to enter and manifest our current experience of life upon earth, is also clearly perceivable in what we may call The Seven Year Cycle.

EMOTIONAL:
During the first seven years of our life, we are called children. During childhood, it is accepted that we are for the most part emotional beings. We are literally energy spontaneously in motion.

MENTAL:
Around the age of seven, we depart childhood and are then called young boys and girls. As young boys and girls, we enter an educational institution intended to direct our awareness into the mental body. We are taught to read, write, count, and communicate efficiently through a set of prescribed letters and numbers.

PHYSICAL:
After another seven years, around the age of fourteen, we are no longer called boys and girls; we are teenagers. As teenagers, we experience a physiological transformation within our physical body, marking an entry into a more physically magnified experience. We call this physical transformation puberty. After puberty, there is a definite shift in our relationship with our physical experience. This is evident, for example, in our relationship with our sexuality. Before puberty, a young boy's or girl's approach to adults kissing is "Yuck!" Afterward, there is deep attraction to the experience.

After another seven years, we turn 21 and are no longer regarded as teenagers. We are called young adults. To commemorate our arrival at adulthood, and the completion of this cyclic journey from childhood (emotional) to teenager (mental) to adult (physical), we usually celebrate. We celebrate because in this moment some part of our journey is completed—and yet another aspect is simultaneously commencing.

The Right Passageway

THERE have been periods upon earth when we were acutely aware of The Pathway of Awareness and The Seven-Year Cycle.

During these periods, communities were intimately involved in facilitating their members along The Pathway of Awareness so that the integrity of their awareness was maintained as they passed through the first three Seven Year Cycles. This conscious facilitation along The Pathway of Awareness took place when we were aligned with our indigenous nature—when we embraced the realm of nature as our teacher.

It is beneficial to reach within and bring our indigenous nature back into the forefront of our conscious awareness—not with intent to return to it, but to integrate it. By integrating our indigenous nature, we are able to make the shift from our attachment to the outer teacher, form, to the inner teacher, vibration. Making this shift consciously and experientially is the leap that reveals to us the evolutionary purpose of humanity.

We may effortlessly integrate our indigenous nature by the telling of a story. We tell a story reminding us of the right passageway for our awareness to move along as it enters an experience of this earth. This right passageway may also be called a rite of passage. *Alchemy of the Heart* is a rite of passage.

The Naming Ceremony

LET us tell the story of a rite of passage as we may experience it when consciously embracing our indigenous nature. This is the story of The Naming Ceremony. "Ceremony" in the phonetic language contains within it the camouflaged phrase *see a memory*.

When a child is born within a community that embraces indigenous awareness, it is not given just any name. For instance, it is not given a name chosen physically, in recognition of its ancestral lineage. Neither is it given a name chosen mentally by selecting it from a list in a book. Nor is it given a name chosen emotionally by selecting a name intended to gratify the self-importance of certain family members.

Communities that embrace their indigenous awareness real eyes that a child's *entry* into life is intimately a part of *every* facet of the life it is entering into. Its birth moment is therefore not perceived as separate from unfolding social conditions, from the movement of the seasons, or from the rainbow of ever-changing faces any aspect of the cosmos expresses at that precise moment. The child is therefore given a name that reflects the personality of the moment in which it exits the womb and enters life upon earth. The child may therefore be named Strange Wind, or Many Crows, or First Dew.

For the most part, this child grows up being overseen by all adults. From birth, it is allowed to be spontaneous energy-in-motion so that it may fully explore and integrate the parameters of its emotional body. Also, by carefully observing the way the child's energy moves, the elders are able to recognize whether this child is the return of someone they know.

When the child turns seven and becomes a young boy or girl, another naming ceremony is conducted. This time it is given a name reflecting what has been witnessed about the way its energy moves upon the earth within its first seven years. It may receive a name like Flowing Water, or Gentle Turtle, or Wind In Grass.

At this point the elders begin applying their responsibility as teachers of the children. In such a community, it is the parents' task to collectively nurture and protect all the children, but it is accepted that young child-bearing adults do not yet have the wisdom to educate children. Wisdom within indigenous communities therefore flows from elder to grandchild.

Once a new name is given to a seven-year-old, the young boy or girl is no longer permitted to run freely around the fire at night. They are instructed to sit and pay attention to the stories told by elders. These stories activate their conscious entry into the development and integration of the mental body.

At the age of about fourteen, the young boys and girls are considered ready to approach adulthood, and this moment is marked by another naming ceremony. During this occasion, the given name reflects what the elders perceive about their mental capacity. The children may therefore receive names such as Sees Gently, or Listens Like Mountain, or Knows Like Eagle.

At this point, the emerging young adults are taught and given physical responsibilities within the community, serving to deliver them confidently along the passageway from young boys and girls to competent and responsible men and women. Many of the tasks involve general living skills, but each individual is also given responsibilities carefully selected according to their unique display of mental capacity.

To mark the transition from a focus on mental activity to increased physical participation within the community, their body awareness is impacted. They go through ceremonial experiences in which their physical body is marked by painting, piercing, and tattooing.

At the age of 21, the young men and women are given a final name— the name they carry with them throughout their journey into elderhood. This name reflects the way they carry themselves through their physical, mental, and emotional experience. The name may be anything from Runs Like Deer, to Wild War Horse, to Laughs Like Smoke.

The Vision Quest

DURING the final naming ceremony, the individual is completely removed from the presence of the community and enters an experience called a vision quest. Among the many rites of passage this ceremony involves, two initiations in particular are carried out:

— I —

The initiate has their awareness expanded beyond the perceptual confines of their mundane experience. This is accomplished through a physical practice like dancing rhythmically all night, or by the ingesting of plant medicines as administered by the medicine elder. The intent of this initiation is to empower, through direct experience, a *trance mission* to the individual that it is not only a member of a community but also an intimate participant in the entire cosmos.

— 2 —

The initiate is taken to an isolated area where a circle is drawn around them in the ground, or constructed using stones, whereupon they are instructed to remain within its confines until fetched. They are left alone for four or five days with only water to drink. The intent of this initiation is to empower the individual to have a direct experience of their own energy—an encounter with their own vibrational state of being. As our purpose is a state of being and not something we do, this energetic encounter with the vibrational essence of their own being facilitates the attaining of a vision of their life's purpose.

When the individual is reintroduced into the community, they enter with the awareness of their purpose within that community, simultaneously interwoven with an awareness of their intimate connection with the entire cosmos. This deliberately invited and instilled vision fosters a profound sense of personal and community-based responsibility. This initiation into adulthood is also the foundation upon which all other experiences mature in a manner that equips the individual to navigate their life experience towards the mantle of elderhood.

Consciously—Or Not

THE nature of our human experience is that we continue to do what we are supposed to do whether we are aware we are doing it or not.

Teenagers unconsciously know they are supposed to impact or mark their physical body in some way to acknowledge the movement of their awareness from mental to physical. Accordingly, they tattoo and pierce their body. Without an authentic elder's guidance, teenagers may turn this piercing and tattooing ceremony into a statement of rebelliousness, as well as into a means to sedate and control inner discomfort. In this way a rite of passage, a sacred act, becomes reactionary behavior and an addictive fashion-statement.

When completing their third seven-year cycle, emerging adults intuitively know they are supposed to move away from their community and enter a ceremony to alter their consciousness. Accordingly, they move away from the presence of adults, buy a keg of beer, maybe obtain mind-altering drugs, have a party, and become intoxicated.

In other words, lacking the guidance of elders, emerging adults now become unconsciously intoxicated in the very moment when they are required to consciously experience the power of their inner altar. A potential experience of Holy Communion becomes an entry into self-destructive confusion.

Without elders, the children of this earth are lost in the wilderness. Yet, we do what we are supposed to whether we are aware that we are doing it or not. If we do not know why we are doing what we are doing, then we do it unconsciously.

Rites of passage entered consciously *integrate*. Rites of passage entered unconsciously *disintegrate*.

Our Unconscious Prayers

A YOUNG man is walking through a desert with an elder. They have been walking for hours through the isolated beauty of the wilderness, when they come upon a large and unusual rock outcrop. It is marked unflatteringly with graffiti and surrounded by shards of smashed beer bottles.

"This is a sacred place," the elder states with reverence. "We must stop here for a moment and lay down a prayer with some tobacco."

"Sacred!" the young man objects. "Look at it. It's a mess!"

"Yes, it is sacred," the elder states softly. "People come upon this place and feel the energy emanating from it. Though a voice they no longer know is speaking to them, they real eyes it is an *altar* and that they are supposed to acknowledge it—to be *altered* by it."

The elder continues in a quiet voice, "But there are few elders left to teach us these ways. So, instead we behave in the only way we know how. We drink beer, mark the rocks with our confused symbols, and smash the bottles to express our rage. Instead of *acting our age,* we *act out our rage.* Our sacred prayers have become destructive spells that we unconsciously cast upon the earth."

The elder carefully takes a pinch of tobacco from his pouch and offers it to the ground. "Let us stand here, together, and say something of power for this place."

‹ 3 ›

The Stories We Tell

A MAN called Frank lives next door to a successful rabbit breeder. The rabbit breeder breeds many admired rabbits, but there is one particular specimen called Fluffy of which he often speaks glowingly. Fluffy is the most beautiful prize-winning rabbit he has bred. Fluffy is also a stud siring large numbers of valuable offspring. Even more importantly, Fluffy is the heart and soul of his daughter's life. His daughter begins and ends each day with Fluffy in her arms.

This morning Frank awakens to discover something shocking hanging from his dog's mouth. He reaches down to gently prize Fluffy's limp, soiled, and saliva-covered body from Rover's jaws. He stands there momentarily paralyzed as a sense of deep panic washes through every vein in his body.

Then, in his thoughts, a story begins: "The neighbor is going to kill me for sure. His daughter is going to go through multiple doses of irreparable childhood trauma, all because my stupid dog has killed Fluffy. In ten years time she will still be in therapy. Rover has just destroyed a peaceful neighborhood. I am in deep trouble. I must *do* something."

Frank examines Fluffy closely and finds no puncture marks from Rover's teeth. He assumes Fluffy died of fright when Rover caught him. He creeps to the fence and peeks over to where Fluffy's cage rests, and there he sees as plain as the dawning day that the cage door is wide open. *Rover must somehow have opened the door,* he tells himself, *and grabbed the poor, defenseless creature.* It is unlike Rover to behave like this, but no other scenario surfaces within Frank's mind. What is he to do?

It is still early and Frank can see his neighbors haven't stirred yet. A brilliant but desperate idea surfaces. Frank rushes into his bathroom with Rover close behind. He takes out his best shampoo and conditioner, then gives the dead rabbit the finest hair treatment any rabbit, dead or alive, ever received. Next, he blow-dries the limp body until it looks beautifully "fluffy" again, just as any prize show rabbit should. Then, for the final step, he fetches a carrot from the fridge, silently climbs the fence into his neighbor's yard, and gently places Fluffy back in his cage, sitting him perfectly upright with a half-eaten carrot stuck in his mouth. He closes and latches the door, then hastily returns to his house. The neighbor will assume Fluffy died choking on a carrot. Disaster has been averted.

Frank makes himself a cup of coffee, then eats breakfast. About an hour later, he is in his yard filling Rover's water bowl for the day when he hears his neighbor scream. Then he hears his neighbor's wife scream. Then he hears their daughter become completely hysterical. Then he hears all three of them screaming together.

Frank observes his neighbors gathered around Fluffy's cage. He wants to run and hide, but his distraught neighbors catch sight of him. To avoid appearing suspicious, Frank walks casually toward them with a concerned look on his face. The breeder, shaking his head from side to side, pale as a sheet, comes over to meet him at the fence.

"What's going on?" Frank asks, trying to sound convincingly curious but not overly concerned.

"I really don't know," blurts his neighbor, looking dazed, confused, bewildered, and somewhat horrified. "Late last night Fluffy died in my daughter's arms from tick bite fever, and then we buried him under a foot of soil in the back yard."

The Art of Magic

THE story about Frank illustrates what happens when we rely solely on the mental and physical aspects of our human experience as the medium to interpret what is unfolding in our lives.

The approach of *thinking we understand what is happening according to what we physically see unfolding in front of us* is what causes us to become "mental" about everything. It is the source of all drama.

Our journey into becoming mental about everything commences when we are children and gathers momentum when we become institutionalized—that is, as we enter the institution called education.

Whether we are aware of it or not, from the moment we embark upon schooling, we are indoctrinated into the art of magic. In fact, we are taught how to become master magicians. The very first lesson we receive is how to *spell words*. Words are the roots of all spells—this is why we have to learn how to *spell* them.

Once we are able to *spell* enough words, we are then taught to arrange them to construct *sentences*. These arrangements of words called *sentences* are our curses and incantations. They *sentence* us and others to specific perceptual points of view. These *sentences* or points of view become the foundation of all our belief systems.

Once we have learned enough sentences, we are then taught *stories*. These are always *his* story—history. History is the mental body's version of reality. History is always written by victors or victims, and victors and victims always lie—that is, report from a point of view that is inherently biased.

The moment we accept any given history, any point of view, we automatically become mental. This is because, through acceptance of the story we are told, we simultaneously accept the means whereby the story is communicated to us—the magical use of words and sentences to convey specific mental perceptions. We then use the same technique, the same magical art, the same spelled words and sentences to tell ourselves stories about *what we think is happening, or has happened, to us.*

The stories we tell ourselves become *my* story—the mystery. *My story* is purely a mental interpretation of the physical events happening within our life experience. This story does not include the emotional component and is therefore incomplete.

In this manner, our every mental interpretation becomes a doorway to misinterpretation. Like Frank, we tell stories based on a mental analysis of our physical circumstances. We then act upon our conclusions and assumptions—and this in turn feeds an ongoing drama that is both comic and tragic.

This "spellbinding" predicament is one perspective on the symbol of the snake eating its tail. The symbol mirrors our propensity for digesting the tales we tell ourselves.

Inviting Integration

WE also have the capacity to untangle ourselves from the story we have told by telling ourselves another story, this time an integrated story intended to deliberately bring us into full awareness.

When wielded with *deliberate intent,* the same magical ability we use every moment to entrap ourselves in drama has the capacity to liberate us. This is because the deliberate wielding of our intent to *activate integrated awareness* automatically awakens the emotional component that is missing from our purely physical and mental interpretations.

Once we consciously engage our life experience from a physical, mental, *and* emotional point of view, we enter into *wholeness,* or *integration.* As the phonetics of these words suggest, to become *whole* again is to become Holy, and to *integrate* is to move into greatness.

This unweaving of a spell to regain an awareness of our wholeness is another perspective on the symbol of the snake eating its tail. We swallow ourselves whole to digest the truth.

Karma and Consequences

LET us begin this unweaving of our victim and victor spells with the issue of karma. We have all heard the expression, and may even have used it ourselves, "This is our bad karma." Or, "This is our good karma."

Karma is another word for consequence. Everything is consequence, and therefore everything is karma. We label consequences "good" or "bad" depending on the current story we are telling ourselves. When consequences appear to fit our story, they are "good." But when they interrupt the flow of our story, they are "bad."

There is an element of accuracy in the statement that what is happening to us is either our bad karma or our good karma. However, one of the barometers that shows us we are moving into a deepening awareness is when it starts becoming apparent to us that *what we used to call our good karma is entrapment in unconsciousness,* and *what we used to call our bad karma is actually the key to our liberation into integrated awareness.*

Beyond the confines of the story we tell ourselves about *what we think* is going on, there really are no good or bad consequences. *There are just consequences, and all consequences are just.*

A question well worth asking is: Where is this good and bad karma stored? Where is the causal point of the unfolding consequences that determine the resonances of the physical, mental, and emotional components of our life experience?

Physically Trance Fixed

By the time we are considered adults, we perceive the world in a particular way.

When asked to recount the experiences we call our past, we do so by offering a chronological accumulation of ever-changing physical events and circumstances. This perception of our life as an accumulation of physical events and circumstances means we have entered a physically trance fixed point of view. We now look out upon a world that appears physically solid and inanimate to us, a world in which everything *matters*.

Yet, when we observe the eyes of a newborn child, it is obvious they perceive the world very differently. Judging by the way their eyes move upon their surroundings, it is as if they have no point of focus—as if all they look upon is in constant movement. Their world appears to them as constant *energy in motion*.

Quantum physicists tell us there really is no solid, static, and lifeless matter—that everything, no matter how solid and inanimate it appears to be, is alive with constant movement.

Why does an adult require a powerful microscope to real eyes what a newborn child experiences effortlessly?

Felt-Perception

THE reason we perceive the world as inanimate—as solid and life-less—is that by the time we are adults, we are physically trance fixed. We are physically trance fixed because our heart awareness is shut down.

Heart awareness is felt-perception. Felt-perception is the ability to feel the consequences of our thoughts, words, and deeds *even before we put them into play.*

When we function from the capacity of felt-perception and we in-tend to hurt someone, *we feel hurt* before even acting upon this intent. When we function from the capacity of felt-perception, the nature of our presence upon earth is therefore guided intimately by our heart.

This is the meaning of the ancient statement, "Where there is love, there is no law." We only require laws when we cannot feel the con-sequences of our behavior.

This capacity to feel is also the perceptual attribute enabling us to perceive that there is life, and therefore movement, in everything. When we live with our felt-perception shut down or diminished, we forgo the fullness of the experience that life upon earth has to offer.

No Conscience

WE have our heart awareness shut down between the ages of seven and fourteen. Because of this, it would be impossible and quite intolerable for us, as we are now, to function efficiently in our lives if we instantly activated full-blown felt-perception within the adult world as we experience it.

It would be too painful because the consequences of our thoughts, words, and deeds—especially as they are currently unfolding within our unconsciousness—are hurtful.

For example, functioning from felt-perception makes it intolerable to mine the earth out of greed, unbearable to manipulate others just for profit, and inconceivable to imprison animals in concentration camps for the production of food.

By the time we are adults, we function primarily from thought-perception, with our thoughts hypnotically fixated upon the seemingly inanimate appearance of our previously animated experience. In other words, we have moved from an internal vibrational experience of life that is felt to a physicalized external experience that is thought about. This perceptual condition constantly leads us to turn our attention outward, away from any felt-insight about our authentic emotional condition.

As long as we are perceptually externalized in this state of felt-numbness, it is easy to mentally justify any physical behavior. In this state of felt-paralysis, we have little or no access to the resonance of what we mentally call conscience, which is the ability to feel the consequences of our presence upon earth. While functioning from a physically trance fixed point of view, our version of conscience is a mentally-driven concept and the exhibiting of a pre-determined, rule-restricted, physical model of behavior.

Where Is Our Past?

BY the time we have become adults, perceptually our life experience constitutes *all that matters.*

When we then *look back* upon our life experience, we perceive it as an accumulated sequence of physical events and circumstances that have unfolded up to this moment. Accordingly, the past appears to us as something outside of us, because this is the assumption behind all physical events and circumstances—they are happening "outside of us."

There is a perceptual error in perceiving the past as something behind us, something that we can look back on, something outside of us. The past is not behind us. No matter how often and how quickly we physically turn around, we cannot see a past *behind* us.

Our past is also not outside of us. Aside from the scattering of objects we surround ourselves with that come from our past, when we look around, we do not see the events of our past outside of us—we only see their consequences.

For instance, we cannot see the experience we call our childhood as something happening out there upon the earth. We can only see its consequences. This is because the past is not behind us or outside us. The past is *inside* us, radiating outwardly as our current circumstances.

If we are able to accept that the causal punctuations of the events that make up the experiences we call our past are contained within us, then what is "our past" currently made of?

Nothing Is Happening

WHEN we do not function from felt-perception, we look *back upon our past* as something that happened *outside of us*, something to which we have attached a story. It therefore appears to us that our past is an accumulation of constantly changing physical events and circumstances.

This appearance of constant change is because the physical aspect of our experience is also a master magician. It is constantly changing its form. Constant change is its constant. Each dawning day *appears* different, and this constant changing of physical appearance leads us to assume each day is new, and that within each *new* day, we are having a *new* experience.

Each day we awaken, and the weather is adjusted, while people are standing in different places dressed in different clothing. We eat different food and attend different activities. We perform different tasks at different times. This leads us to assume our life is a constantly changing series of events and circumstances. This appearance of each day being a new one, because it *looks* different, is a story we tell ourselves that is supported by the ever-changing appearances of form—the slight of hand of our physical experience.

Yet, a deception underlies this *appearance of change*. Awareness of this deception stirs whenever we think or say something like, "Why does this keep happening to me?"

An uncomfortable truth slithering beneath this illusion of constant change is also reflected back to us whenever we attempt to adjust our physical circumstances, or our thoughts about something, in an effort to change the quality of our experience.

From within the appearance of constant change smiles a hidden truth. It smiles at us as our inevitable reentry into the same frequency of inner felt-discomfort from which we have repeatedly attempted to mentally and physically liberate ourselves.

If our life is truly ever-changing, ever-new, then why do we experience boredom? The feeling of boredom is a clue that, despite all the outer activity—despite all our mental and physical efforts to change the quality of our experience—nothing really happens or changes.

Something only *appears* to be happening or changing.

‹ 4 ›

The Vibrational

THE word *vibrational* is used within this text instead of the word *spiritual* because the word spiritual is as emotionally-charged as it is vague. The word *vibrational* on the other hand hints at something that is crucial when intending to enter a conversation with the unspeakable—the importance of *feeling*.

The word spiritual, because it is already so conceptually encased, may cause unintentional segregation. The moment we identify ourselves as "a spiritual person," we may unconsciously be making an assumption that there are others upon this earth who are not spiritual. But who isn't spiritual? Only when we are physically trance fixed and caught up in constant mental interpretation of our experiences do we perceive that some people are of spirit while others are not.

By defining ourselves as a spiritual person, we may also open ourselves to the error of adopting specific behaviors we assume are characteristic of spiritual people. Then, when a moment arises in which we are called upon to behave authentically, if this required behavior is not within our definition of what constitutes being a spiritual person, we are trapped. We cannot behave authentically because "it is not spiritual." Perceiving ourselves as a spiritual person can therefore make us vulnerable to the perceptual confusion our entry into so-called spirituality is intended to liberate us from.

The word vibrational is free of all this mental and emotional baggage. It is neutral. A vibrational experience is a felt-encounter, not a mental understanding we come to, or a physical behavior we have to adopt or portray. Therein is the master clue as to how we are to approach a conversation with the unspeakable.

Being In the Womb

WE have discussed how The Pathway of Awareness moves from the *emotional* resonance of childhood, through the *mental* stage of our teenage years, and then into the *physical* trance fixed encounters of our adulthood.

However, this energetic pathway does not begin at the moment of birth and the start of the emotional period of childhood. It commences within the womb as a vibrational resonance.

The essence of a vibrational state is *being*. This is also why the womb experience may be considered a vibrational experience for us. We can do nothing in the womb aside from *be*.

While in the womb, our being is immersed in vibrations—in the sum of the vibrations we experience through our mother's beating heart, blood pumping, lungs breathing, vocal tone, body temperature, body posture, and so on.

Our exit from the womb marks a transition point from being to doing.

The First Cycle of Seven

WE do not immediately enter the womb at the moment of conception. The physical vehicle we call our body first goes through a period of development empowering it with the capacity to contain the immensity of our vibrational essence.

Our awareness only enters the physical body at about two months into the nine-month pregnancy cycle. We are therefore in the womb for a period of seven months. This seven-month experience in the womb is our first seven cycle.

We may therefore call this seven-month womb experience the initial vibrational aspect that inaugurates our journey along The Pathway of Awareness. Seen from its point of inauguration, the journey we take along The Pathway of Awareness as we enter our experience upon this earth moves from vibrational (womb) to emotional (childhood) to mental (teenage) to physical (adult).

Imprinting

THE word imprinting within the text of this book refers to the deliberate transference of energetic data which occurs within the first twenty-one years of our life experience—within the first emotional, mental, and physical seven-year cycles.

Because the transference of this data is energetic, in the midst of its unfolding, the actual procedure of imprinting is practically impossible to perceive by the individual being imprinted. So as we move beyond the first three seven-year cycles into becoming mentally and physically trance fixed by our experience, the presence and impact of this imprinting upon the quality of our human experience remains hidden.

The intent of this energetic transference is to systematically imprint our emotional, then mental, and then physical body with specific data that we can access when we attain the capacity to adjust it. Imprinting is like energetic tattooing. It may also be thought of as the downloading of consequences into the emotional, mental, and physical components of our human experience, or the grounding into this life of karma from previous life experiences.

Imprinting commences while we are in the womb as an energetic transmission—a vibrational pattern delivered to us through the intricacies of our mother's experience. It then continues to unfold as a felt-impression within the first seven years of our life after birth, as a mental-impression (telling stories) from seven to fourteen years of age, and then as a physical-impression between fourteen to 21 years of age.

From the age of twenty-one onward, our life experience is overshadowed and underlined by this imprinted pattern—and remains so until we awaken to it and consciously interact with it.

Vibrational Transmission

As a means of illustrating this imprinting procedure, we shall journey through the various stages of the experience using a fictitious series of events. We will tell a story intended to assist us to consciously integrate the imprinting procedure. In the telling of this story, we will examine the dynamics and impact of an imprinted event, or downloaded piece of energetic data, that reoccurs with the regularity of our seven-year cycles.

The telling of this story gradually reveals how an imprinted experience becomes an unseen causal point of the repetitious nature of many of the uncomfortable aspects of our life experience. In other words, imprinting is the answer to the question, "Why does this keep happening to me?"

We commence our story by beginning within the womb experience—the vibrational aspect of The Pathway of Awareness. To serve the purpose of this illustration, we are going to examine an event that is repeatedly imprinted at the six-year point along the vibrational, emotional, mental, and physical seven-year cycles.

Imprinting of Abandonment

LET us suppose that an incident takes place in the eighth month of our mother's pregnancy. Our mother and father have a heated dispute. They married each other, turned each other into each other's parents, and now cannot stand being together. After all, who wants to sleep with their parents?

In the wake of a nasty emotional fight, our father walks out. In this moment there is a powerful emotional resonance we may conceptually call abandonment. Our father abandons our mother, and our mother feels abandoned by our father. This resonance of abandonment is made up of an emotional salad containing the ingredients of fear, anger, and grief.

Fear, anger, and grief are the trinity of all emotional dysfunction.

Fear relates directly to the physical. It is a reaction to the threatening of our physical mortality. Anger relates directly to the mental— revenge is a plot! Grief relates directly to the emotional body.

While in the womb, we do not experience the frequency of abandonment as the emotions of fear, anger, and grief, but rather as powerful vibrations. Our mother's experience throughout this emotional encounter is transmitted to us vibrationally through the way her physical condition mirrors her emotional encounter within the heat of the moment.

As this emotional encounter between our mother and father unfolds, the resonance of abandonment penetrates our awareness through the way our mother's heart beats, the way she breathes, the way her blood pumps. It is in the tone of her voice as she expresses, and in the movement of her physical frame. Consequently, the complexity of the emotional signature beneath the experience of abandonment impacts our vibrational awareness in a precise manner.

A Deliberate Signal

THE vibrational body is different from the emotional, mental, and physical bodies, in that the emotional, mental, and physical bodies can be imprinted—temporarily altered—whereas the vibrational cannot.

The vibrational body simply transmits a signal. Once the signal has passed through, there is no record left of the transmission.

Our seven-month womb experience is used to transmit and carry a signal vibrationally from our previous incarnation to the incarnation we are now intending. This signal is deliberately carried by the vibrational through the womb as experiences mirrored through our mother while we are in the womb. In other words, our mother's experience during pregnancy is a deliberately staged multi-dimensional experience containing the raw data of the seeds of our potential.

During the first seven years of our life, this vibrational transmission is deliberately deposited into our emotional body as distinct energetic patterns.

As long as we are physically trance fixed by our experience, we do not have the capacity to perceive the absolute deliberateness of this imprinting experience. Accordingly, it appears as if everything is happening randomly, chaotically, and meaninglessly. The reason it appears so is that the entire imprinting experience is one of energy in motion—an energetic unfolding whose deliberateness we cannot perceive while we lack emotional body awareness.

Imprinting the Emotional

As we depart the womb, the vibrational signal we have received is systematically discharged by being imprinted as a pattern, like a tattoo, into the emotional body.

To get a picture of this imprinting procedure, we continue with our illustration. We now move from the abandonment experience between our mother and father that occurred eight months into our womb experience, to when we are six years old, which is six years along our first seven-year cycle after birth.

Our parents have attempted to patch things up and stay together for the sake of the child. But the reality is that they cannot stand the sight of each other. They are clearly reflecting each other's unintegrated issues. But because they are both physically trance fixed and lack emotional body awareness, they believe they must resolve matters by changing the other person through discussion, debate, and the request of "conditions," instead of looking within. This leads them to a dead-end situation—divorce.

As the divorce proceedings unfold, we as a six-year-old interact with this event primarily through our emotional body. We do not yet have the mental conceptual capacity to know what the word divorce means, nor the accumulated physical life experience to contain what a divorce proceeding between two people entails in any manner that is integrated. For us, it is predominantly an emotional experience—an encounter with uncomfortable feelings.

As our mother and father move through this experience, for us it means the surfacing of a resonance of abandonment, containing the emotional salad of fear, anger, and grief. Through our child's experience of felt-perception, this resonance of abandonment is now imprinted into our emotional body. Consequently, it dictates the way our energies "move in motion." More accurately, it sets up a condition in which certain aspects of our energetic system *no longer move freely in motion*. This becomes our emotional blueprint.

Imprinting the Mental

WE fast-forward another seven years to the age of thirteen, six years along our second seven-year cycle after birth. We now live with our mother in a neighborhood in which we have become close friends with one particular individual. Because we now clearly have abandonment issues, we cling almost obsessively to this person. They are our declared "best, best, best, best friend!"

One day our best friend's parents are informed that they are being transferred out of state, and within two weeks our companion is ripped out of our reality. We again experience the resonance of abandonment, which is made of the emotional salad containing fear, anger, and grief. However, even though this impacts us as a powerful emotional experience, we do not encounter it as such.

By now we have been going to school, where we are taught magic. Consequently, we interact with this experience mentally—conceptually. We engage with this event by *telling ourselves a story* about who we are and about the nature of the world we live in. Through this story, we are establishing our belief system. This becomes "my story," the weaving of the mystery. Through this storytelling, the resonance of abandonment is tattooed into our mental body.

Imprinting the Physical

WE fast-forward another seven years to the age of twenty, six years along our third seven-year cycle after birth. We are now a young adult, deeply in love with someone, standing at the altar in a church waiting for them to arrive. The fact is, we now have acutely deep-set abandonment issues, and therefore asked this person to marry us three days after our first date.

We wait eagerly at the altar. This promises to be the most wonderful day of our life so far. We look at our watch repeatedly as the minutes tick slowly by. Eventually, it dawns on us that we have been ditched at the altar. We again enter the resonance of abandonment, a salad made up of fear, anger, and grief.

Even though we display strong emotional reactions to what is unfolding, it is not primarily an emotional experience for us. Even though we again tell ourselves a story about what is going on in that moment, it is no longer primarily a mental experience for us.

By the age of twenty, our awareness is firmly trance fixed by the physical components of our experience. Consequently, the experience of abandonment is now primarily a physical circumstance or predicament, and we voice it as such: "How dare *she* do this to *me* on *this day* with all these people here?" We perceive the resonance of abandonment according to the physical circumstances in which we now find ourselves. In this way the resonance of abandonment is tattooed into the physical aspect of our experience.

"Why Does This Keep Happening to Me?"

WE again fast forward seven years to the age of twenty-seven. We are now a successful young professional. We entered a field of study for four years and exited with a qualification that enabled us to gain lucrative employment.

Because we are extremely needy and have powerful underlying abandonment issues, we worked really hard, lived through a life of late nights, schmoozing with the right people, wearing the right clothes, and being seen in the right places.

During an evening's encounter of loose-tongued cocktail banter, our boss insinuates that we are the right person for a position opening at the end of the month. Our neediness makes this drunken talk believable to us.

On the day of the promotion announcement, our boss gives the position to the person in the office next to us—a person we assumed was our best friend. We are devastated. We are also embarrassed because we told everyone we were going to be promoted.

Underneath the tidal wave of anxiety we are feeling runs the resonance of abandonment. We *feel* abandoned by our boss, by our best friend in the next office, by our years of study, and by all our social efforts.

Even though we are emotionally distraught and mentally imploding, it is on the physical circumstances that our focus is now concretely trance fixed. We ask ourselves, "How can this be happening to me? How dare the boss let me down? Look at how hard I worked for him! What was it all for?"

At this point, we may ask a question that holds the clue to the causal point of our personal turmoil. If we ask it sincerely, it has the capacity to assist us to real eyes what is really unfolding. The question is, "Why *does* this keep happening to me?"

Emotionally Blinded

WE feel like we are cursed and cannot understand why. We work hard. We try our best. Yet, in the moment when it really counts, we appear to be sabotaged by unseen forces. "Life is not fair," we declare.

When we look *back* upon our life through eyes now concretely trance fixed upon the accumulation of physical events and circumstances from which we tell our story, it appears as if our life experience is an ever-changing mishap of bad luck. Because of the slight of hand of the physical aspect of our experience—its ability to dress each day up differently—we cannot see that *since we were seven years old, nothing new has ever happened to us.*

We cannot real eyes this because we no longer view our life upon earth through eyes that can perceive the causal point of our experience—the eyes of realization that perceive energy-in-motion.

Our physical eyes can now only show us the various forms our initial childhood experiences have been shaped into, and these physical manifestations are constantly changing because the only constant of the physical aspect of our experience is that it constantly changes. When we look upon our life experience as an accumulation of physical events and circumstances, we are blind to what stays the same. Our physical eyes cannot perceive anything that remains unchanged. Yet, often when we enter states of discomfort, a niggling voice within our awareness whispers to us of *something* that never seems to change.

Our mental eyes of understanding are just as blind because they only perceive the story we have told ourselves about what is happening to us—a story that contains as much truth as the story Frank told himself about how Fluffy arrived in Rover's mouth. When we then source our behavior from this story, we enter the same level of comic tragedy that Frank did, and unleash the same caliber of drama as he did upon himself and his neighbors. This is the comic tragedy behind a reliance on analysis.

When we mentally *anal eyes* our life, we inevitably enter *assumption,* and end up feeling like an *asshole.*

Once we enter adulthood, our predicament is that we have almost no emotional body awareness and cannot therefore perceive energy-in-motion, with the consequence that we are to a large extent perceptually blinded.

From our perceptually incapacitated state, when we *look back upon* our life—at the divorce of our parents when we were six, at the sudden departure of our best friend when we were thirteen, at the no-show of our fiancé when we were twenty, and at the perceived betrayal by our boss at the age of twenty-seven—all these events appear to be completely separate incidents having nothing in common. They happened at different periods in our life and appear completely unrelated in their unfolding.

Yet, the clue to our tragic predicament arises like the dawning of the sun and offers its light whenever we exclaim with frustration, "Why *does* this keep happening to me?"

In-Sight Out

IF we are able to briefly enter the perceptual capacity inherent in emotional body awareness, we real eyes that beneath each of these seemingly unrelated occurrences is *an identical emotional signature*—a particular emotional salad we now conceptually spell as fear, anger, and grief.

This particular reoccurring, emotionally uncomfortable resonance may now also be summarized in one word—abandonment. But because we are blind to the condition of our emotional body, we cannot get to the heart of the matter.

By the time we are in this adult state and have gone through various repetitions of this echoing Seven-Year Cycle, we have entered a behavioral experience in which everything we perceive is inside out, backwards, and upside down. We cannot connect the emotional dots, and so we behave as if the effect of our experience is the causal point—as if the only way to impact the quality of our experience is to rearrange it physically, or to adjust our mental interpretation of it.

The awareness that these circumstances have something to do with an emotional signature—with energy in motion, or more accurately, with energy *not* in motion—is lost on us.

Once this imprinted abandonment cycle has repeatedly and psychologically impacted us, we do not real eyes that our entire life experience becomes a defensive duel with an unseen emotional signature. Everything we do is a vain physical and mental attempt to counteract our sense of abandonment. We avoid commitment. We do not allow ourselves to get too close to others. We eventually find a job where we are invisible and safe.

In the quiet hours, we try to *think our way* out of our predicament by analyzing it over and over and over with our mental body. We wonder what physical steps we can take to change. Eventually, we give up and "get on with it." We have now become like everyone else—"in effect you all," *ineffectual.*

Our life experience is reduced to activities designed to sedate and control our inner discomfort, which serves to keep from us an awareness of our helplessness.

Emotions Are Weakness

BECAUSE we do not have emotional body awareness, we no longer use our felt-perception as a means of perception. We now use it as a tool for drama—a means to display our fear, anger, and grief.

Our expressions of drama are not an indicator of emotional body awareness. Fear, anger, and grief, when projected outward into the world, are a dysfunction of the emotional body. Our external display of drama is a tool we use to get the attention from others that we are not yet emotionally mature enough to give ourselves.

The physical body grows when we give it the most basic nutrition, so that by the time we are in our twenties, we look physically like an adult. The mental body also develops when we apply ourselves to the most basic mental activities, like learning to read, write, and count.

Yet, after we are seven years old, there is no forum for the conscious or deliberate development of the emotional body. On the contrary, we are just exiting an era in the story of our humanity in which un-inhibited emotional body expression is reserved for children, artists, performers, the eccentric, the gay community, young girls, and the "emotionally unstable." Uninhibited emotional expression in the mental adult world receives the mantle of a sign of weakness, flamboyance, instability, sin, and lack of self-control.

Outwardly, we now observe the consequence of this lack of emotional body development in the behavior of our politicians. When they cannot *get* their way, they behave like seven-year-old children on a school playground.

The lack of emotional body development in the human species impacts every aspect of our adult experience. The Catch-22 of this predicament is that to perceive the causal point and the consequences of this emotional retardation requires emotional body awareness.

Consequently, when life does not unfold according to our story, we adults behave like immature children, and few of us have the capacity to perceive why.

‹ 5 ›

Have a "Nice" Day

B Y the time we are adults, we are unconsciously nursing a consistent and ever-increasing discomfort within our emotional body.
Yet, because we cannot perceive this, we cannot ease it.

We build upon this discomfort by unconsciously embracing reactive
behaviors to compensate for this condition. These reactive behaviors
become our "needs" and "wants." We then unconsciously design our
life experience around feeding an appetite for inner relief that cannot
be satiated because we are not even aware that this is what we are doing.

People ask, "How are you?"

We reply, "Fine, thank you." Or we tell them we are "doing okay."
We then say to them, "Have a nice day."

What do the words *fine, okay,* and *nice* mean? Nothing. These are
emotionally vacant words that arise regularly in our vocabulary when
we are emotionally bankrupt.

Our only hope is to be able to perceive our plight with the eyes of
awareness. It is only our awareness of our predicament that transforms
the unconscious aspects of this experience and saves us from being
condemned to living a "nice" life.

Spell "Live" Backwards

By the time we are adults, through imprinting and example, we have modeled our behavior upon those who continually enter and exit our life experience. Like organic photocopying machines, we duplicate the perceptual predicament of our parents, peers, preachers, politicians, and business leaders.

This behavior is backwards.

We behave as if *the effect is the cause*. In other words, we behave as if the physical world is happening to us, as opposed to it reflecting what is unfolding energetically within us.

When we live backwards, we may describe our perceptual plight by spelling the word "live" backwards.

It is important to neutralize the emotionally charged and religiously ordained baggage transmitted by the word "evil," so that we may awaken from the perceptually hellish predicament encapsulated in this word. It is useful to say the word "evil" out loud and observe what feelings it generates within us. These feelings are a programmed response. They are tied to a story we have told ourselves. They are a *sentence*—the consequence of a *spell*.

Evil behavior is all behavior born of the same perceptual error— perceiving an effect as if it were the cause, and acting accordingly.

Evil Behavior

LET us illustrate "evil behavior," or how we "live backwards," so that we may clearly observe the presence of this perceptual error within our own life experience.

To illustrate how we manifest a circumstance in our life experience, we may use the act of throwing a pen across a room. If we are holding a pen in our hand and we throw it across the room, according to the way we currently behave upon this earth, we believe that if we want to change the way we are throwing the pen, we must go to where it has landed on the ground and move it around at that point.

In other words, if we do not like our body, we physically do something to it. Or if we do not like our partner, we find a new one. Or if we do not like our job, we leave and seek new employment. Or if we do not like the country we live in, we relocate to another.

We behave as if the physical aspect of our experience is the causal point of the quality of our experience. So, when we feel uncomfortable in any way, we initiate activity intended to adjust our physical circumstances.

The Pathway of Awareness reveals that the causal point of energy entering and manifesting upon this earth is the heart. It then moves from the heart into the emotional, through the mental, and into the physical. Consequently, making mental or physical adjustments to ourselves in an attempt to alter the quality of our experience, and thereby improve how we feel, is the same as trying to alter the way the pen is flying through the air, or moving it around on the floor after it has landed, as if such actions could somehow change the way we threw it.

Of course, everyone behaves in this manner, which makes it appear normal. In reality, behaving in this manner is insane.

According to The Pathway of Awareness, the pen, while in our hand, represents the emotional aspect of our experience—the causal point. Then, while it is flying through the air, it is the mental aspect of our experience—the corridor from the emotional into the physical.

Where and in what position it lands on the floor is the physical aspect of our experience—the point of manifestation. To attempt to adjust *the quality of our experience* (how we *feel* about what is happening to us) by rearranging our mental state or physical circumstances is therefore to meddle with the effect in order to make an adjustment at the causal point. This is backwards behavior.

The question is, what hypnotizes us into believing we can alter *how we feel* about an experience by adjusting it physically, or even by altering our mental take on it?

In Effect You All

WHENEVER we feel uncomfortable and react to our experience by physically making adjustments—rearranging our physical circumstances by changing our partner, job, or living circumstances—the same inevitable consequence plays itself out.

Initially, we feel different because our outer physical experience appears to be altered. However, generally within three weeks to three months of making any major physical alteration in our life experience, the same uncomfortable *feeling* that caused us to seek a change in the first place begins surfacing within our awareness.

Even though we have changed the parameters of our physical experience, time reveals that nothing is altered. Our behavior is therefore ineffectual. This is because, according to The Pathway of Awareness, which moves from emotional to mental to physical, our physical circumstances are an *effect* of the original emotional experience that unfolded within the first seven years of our life.

Of course, we cannot perceive this. Why? Because by looking only at the physical aspect of our life experience, we remain blind to the energetic flow that birthed it. We do not real eyes that our outer physical circumstance is always the reflection of something else—an energy that is in motion or an energy that is no longer in motion.

The physical—the aspect of our experience that appears to *matter* the most—is purely an *effect* mirroring the condition of something else currently unseen by us. To alter an effect with the intent of adjusting a cause is to behave backwards. Behaving backwards is ineffectual, *in-effect-you-all*.

As long as we continue to perceive our life as purely a physical occurrence, or as a mental construct that has become manifest physically, our attempt to transform the quality of our experience within it remains ineffectual.

"Making Peace" Is Insanity

LET us examine our backwards behavior from another perspective. Here upon earth, in-effect-you-all behavior is the norm and considered sane.

Our politicians behave this way in every aspect of their administration of government. Our media perceives life upon earth in this way in every aspect of its news coverage. Our many religions behave this way in the manner in which they interact with each other and within the rituals they use to approach what God is for them.

Let us "demon straight" this perceptual error. Currently, there are two ways we approach peace upon earth, and these differ according to what we perceive is the causal point of our experience:

—*1*—

When we believe the causal point of our experience is *the physical,* we behave as our politicians do. If we want to *make peace,* we tell everyone else to "Shut up and sit still!" so that peace may be achieved. If we are not obeyed, we then *enforce peace* by sending in armed forces to confine others in circumstances we deem peaceful. This is the approach of a human who believes peace is a physical circumstance. There is no record in human history of achieving an awareness of peace by enforcing specific physical circumstances on others, and to continue to honor such behavior is insanity. To place the word "force" and the word "peace" in the same sentence is only possible when we are evil.

—*2*—

When we believe the causal point of our experience is *the mental*, we behave like most peacekeeping organizations do. If we want to *make peace,* we invite everyone to bring their written manifesto on what they believe initiates peace, and then we discuss these points until we can agree on a manifesto acceptable to all concerned. Once we are in agreement, we call in the media and publicly sign this document. This is how we behave if we believe peace is a mental concept. There is no record in human history of achieving an awareness of peace by treating it as a mental concept, and to continue to honor such behavior is insanity. To believe we can accomplish peace authentically through "agreement" with others is madness. To behave as if peace arises out of discussion or debate only appears feasible when we are evil.

These two approaches form a macrocosm that reflects the microcosm of how we conduct ourselves within our individual life experience. We treat ourselves, our families, our lovers, our friends, and our communities the same way our politicians and peace organizations behave when we attempt to "make peace" by rearranging physical circumstances or through discussion and agreement.

Both approaches are *in-effect-you-all*.

Making What Already Is

PEACE is not a physical circumstance, although it can be perceived through physical circumstances. Peace is also not a mental concept, although it can be communicated as one, just as we are doing through this text.

Peace, initially, is perceived by us as a feeling.

According to The Pathway of Awareness, when we feel at peace, this feeling radiates automatically from the heart into our energy-in-motion-body (emotional), then into our thought forms (mental), and is then reflected back to us from and through our outer circumstances (physical).

The notion that we have to "make peace" is a perceptual error that breeds delusional behavior. Peace is of the vibrational. It is already a given, not something we have to make. The entire earth is at peace. The region we call The Middle East is and always has been drenched in peace. The whole of Africa is embraced by peace. Our entire planet is enveloped in peace. Simply remove all humans from any war-torn or conflict-ridden environment, and what immediately becomes evident is the immense peace that always is.

It is a gross perceptual error to assume that we have to make peace. We do not have to *make* peace; we have to become aware of the conditions within our current human experience that obscure the peace that already is. Peace is a given. Peace is already part of creation's vibrational resonance, and what is already created does not require recreating.

Awareness Undoes

BECAUSE peace is already a given, we cannot, through physical and mental manipulation—through our "doings"—transform an existing experience into a peaceful, loving, and joyful one. This is like trying to wet water.

Our task is to bring *awareness* to what it is about our current experience that is obscuring our realization of the peace that is always present. Bringing awareness to this perceptual error—to the mistaken assumption that we must make peace—transforms our experience so that we may become vulnerable to effortlessly realizing the peace that already is.

Accomplishing this transformation does not require more "doing." It requires undoing or "not-doing." By realizing the conflicted and perceptually erroneous predicament we are in, and by perceiving the mechanisms that led us into this confusion, we empower ourselves to undo, untangle, and uncover a perceptual spell that has been cast. The story being told in this world—that we have to *make* peace—is a lie. It is an evil spell.

Birthing Our Act

To gain a deeper awareness of how the condition of our emotional body, as it is imprinted within the first seven years of our life, becomes the causal point for our present behavior, we reenter the timeline of the illustration we have been using concerning our journey from childhood into adulthood. As we move through the illustration this time, we observe the unfolding experience from a different perspective. We are not examining imprinting. Instead, we are watching our movement *from presence to pretence,* and noting the consequences this has for our overall behavior.

We commence by returning to our experience as a six-year-old, just prior to our parents' divorce proceedings. One morning, as we are playing in the front hallway of our house, we see visitors arriving. Because of our parents' inability to see anything but their unresolved experiences reflected in each other, our home is currently saturated with emotional heaviness. The site of visitors is a welcome change in the atmosphere. We are overjoyed! Consequently, we jump up and down singing a loud song: "Visitors! Visitors! We have visitors! Visitors are coming!" We dance about the house jubilantly, chanting our joyful song.

As a reaction to our spontaneity, our parents shout, "Quiet down and behave yourself! Can't you see we have visitors arriving?"

Consequently, as the visitors step through the front door, we are standing statue-still, suppressing our energy, now with barely a toe moving. "And this is our child," our parents say, pointing our way.

"Oh!" they exclaim. "What a *well behaved little child you are.*" They lean forward and pat us on the head like a dog, then look back at our parents and say, "You are so blessed to have such a well-behaved child."

This is possibly the most attention we have received all day, or maybe all week—and we receive it *for behaving inauthentically.*

This behavior is *safe*—we remember this. We take note of this moment. We file this particular "act" they call "good behavior" in the favorable memory department. It brought us attention and made us feel special and appreciated. In this moment, our authentic essence withdraws a little and slips into the unseen.

We experience a gradual shift from *presence* to *pretence*.

From this moment onward, our spontaneous joyfulness now triggers the imprinted energetic memory of a reprimand—a resonance that leads us to assume we are not accepted, just as it leads us to assume we are not safe.

From this moment onward, to feel safe and be seen, we willingly take out our act of "good behavior." We reenact it whenever we feel the same resonance of joyfulness arise within us.

Through instances like this, our reactive behavior is born and the seeds of our calculated, pretentious, adult behavior are sown. Our future now holds the promise of us being "a nice person"—a person who says "no" when we mean "yes," and "yes" when we mean "no."

Nice people cannot be trusted because they say and do anything to feel safe and to be accepted.

Becoming the "Cool" Person

WE now fast forward along this timeline to about two years after puberty. We are sixteen years old. We no longer perceive sexuality as a repulsive intrusion; it now attracts us like a powerful magnet.

One day, we are in the hallway at school when we catch the eye of an individual who lives down the road from us. Their physical presence does something strange and completely unexpected to our whole state of being. Whenever we see them, we want to dance around and sing a song that declares, "Whenever I see you, I feel so weird it hurts! But I love the pain and cannot stop looking at you!"

However, as this spontaneous energy arises, our unconscious filing cabinet informs us that in this moment we are to seek safety and acknowledgment, not vulnerability and the potential for embarrassment.

According to the instructions attached to these files, we are to take out our act. As this person passes by, we half-glance at them and barely move the fingers of our right hand as a greeting. "Hey," we say quietly in a calculated monotone, and immediately go on our way. Because our authentic behavior is now deeply suppressed, we have become one of the "cool" people at school.

About a week after this incident, we are standing in the front hallway of our house feeling bored and distracted. To our surprise we see this person walking up the pathway to our front door. Our heart leaps to life, and blood begins pumping to all areas of our body. We want to jump around and dance up and down the passageway declaring, "You are coming to see me! Me, me, me! I am the one! You are coming to see me!" But we do not. We are now unable to be authentic. Spontaneous behavior does not feel safe or acceptable.

Accordingly, we take out our act. We open the door and coolly say, "Hey, what's up? You wanna come in?" Fortunately, this person is equally suppressed and therefore is attracted to this resonance within us. They feel at home in the company of "cool" people.

Resistance, Friction, and Heat

By the time we turn twenty-one and officially enter the adult world, we have almost zero emotional body awareness.

We now only use our emotional body for drama. We often become upset and believe the causes of our upsets are random events happening in our outer experience. We perceive our life experience as something that is happening *to* us, and as something we have to overcome. We have become a victim and a victor.

This behavior appears normal to us because just about everyone within our experience upon earth blames something or someone else when events and circumstances do not go as planned—that is, do not go according to the *story* they are telling.

What we cannot perceive is that by this point in our experience, our emotional body is in great discomfort. It is no longer an energy-in-motion body. It is now mostly an energy-not-in-motion body.

The seeds planted through emotional imprinting within the first seven years of our life are now being harvested as ever-increasing mental confusion and physical discomfort.

We cannot perceive that in the moment we began resisting our authentic behavior and transformed ourselves into a well-behaved little child standing in front of the visitors—instead of the jubilant, chanting, and radiant presence of the universe we had been expressing just prior to their arrival—we transformed the way the energy flows in our emotional body. We resisted its authentic nature.

Something Is Dead

As we journey from childhood through our teenage years, and then into adulthood, we are constantly embracing inauthentic behavior in order to remain "safe" and likeable. Or we embrace rebellious behavior, causing us to get into trouble and be disliked. Or we make ourselves "invisible."

Whatever behavior we use to make it safely from childhood into adulthood is inauthentic and reactive. By the time we are an adult, we are constantly reenacting—resisting our spontaneous urges with calculated acts. This becomes so second nature that we cannot even perceive this about ourselves.

An "adult" is an act, a child in resistance.

When we rub our hands together and simultaneously press them hard into each other to increase resistance while rubbing, the friction that arises between them causes a heat buildup. This is exactly what happens within our emotional body when we resist our authentic behavior—our heart. We go into resistance, which causes friction, which in turn causes a heat buildup.

Because this ongoing mode of resistance causes a constant buildup of heat within our emotional body, we feel increasingly uncomfortable. Yet, we do not feel it directly. This is because, as we make this journey into adulthood, we simultaneously shut down our heart awareness—our capacity to feel.

Initially, we begin shutting down our emotional body awareness by resisting our spontaneous energy in motion. We learn to resist our authentic feelings by metaphorically standing still with only one toe moving when we would rather be jumping for joy.

We do not react directly to the buildup of heat caused by this initial suppression, but we do attend to it indirectly. As we are taught the art of magic at school, we use the words we learn to spell in order to name the various resonances of our inner emotional discomfort. We call them fear, anger, and grief. We use these words to transform our relationship with these uncomfortable feelings of emotional body heat into a conceptual one.

We then double up our resistance to this internal emotional turmoil by suppressing any encounter with the energetic experiences associated with these mental concepts. We suppress all inner awareness of our fear, anger, and grief, until the only evidence of their existence is the chaos and conflict we perceive happening "outside of us."

By the time we are adults, we are allergic to feeling the authentic condition of our emotional body and have externalized any evidence of its condition into activities that appear to be happening *out there,* or *to* us.

By the time we are adults, it is almost impossible for us to perceive that our discomfort is happening *because of us*.

By the time we are adults, something about our experience is dead.

Without In-Sight

WITHOUT heart awareness, we no longer have *in-sight*. In-sight is the ability to see with the eyes of the heart.

This lack of in-sight is what shuts down any awareness of our inner discomfort. It shuts down our ability to perceive from where this discomfort is arising. And it shuts down our ability to perceive that our outer discomfort is a reflection of our inner condition.

This inner condition then leaks, unseen, outward along The Pathway of Awareness. It radiates from within our emotional body into our thought forms, polluting our mental activity. Then it becomes manifest within our behavioral traits, within our bodily condition, and as reoccurring events and circumstances in our life that appear to deliberately sabotage our plans.

Because we do not have emotional body awareness—the ability to perceive energy in motion—we cannot connect the dots. We cannot perceive that the discomfort manifesting in our outer experiences is intimately connected to the inner condition of our emotional body. It appears as if these outer circumstances are unfolding randomly, chaotically, and unfairly.

When we no longer have *in-sight*, we are only able to perceive our life experience as something that is happening *out-sight*—outside. Our life becomes "inside out." We therefore live backwards—we become evil. And that which stands between this condition and us perceiving it is called a "veil."

There is an interesting relationship between the words live, evil, and veil.

Turning Up the Heat

THERE are many, many instances strewn throughout our childhood in which we moved into resistance as a means to feel safe and acknowledged. Now, as a young adult, our emotional body is riddled with resistance, while our outer behavior is polluted with reactive, calculated acts. Consequently, our emotional body is as hot as hell.

Yet, because we have no in-sight, we cannot perceive this, let alone have any awareness of the causal point of this experience. All we know is that sometimes we feel as if we are going to "blow our top" or "lose our cool," or that we need to "blow off some steam."

The well-behaved little child became the cool teenager. The cool teenager became the nice adult. And this predicament is driving us insane. Consequently, over the years we develop behaviors assisting us to *compensate* for this unseen yet all-enveloping inner discomfort. We do not even know that we are compensating. Because our emotional body is the causal point of the quality of our human experience, and because it has been impacted through imprinting and is therefore unconscious to us, most of the reasons that we do what we do are unconscious to us.

The behaviors we unconsciously develop to compensate for our discomfort are our means of sedation and control. We resort to these behaviors because no one can assist us with our internal condition. How can anyone assist us with a predicament that is invisible to the majority of the population of the earth? No one can assist us because only those who real eyes what is happening to them can shed in-sight into what is happening to us.

When these spontaneous energies arise within our emotional body, we no longer perceive them as jubilance. We now unconsciously expect the possibility of reprimand and embarrassment. We feel exposed and unsafe. We are afraid.

Instead of jubilance, we now *spell* this same energetic occurrence "fear," and the frustration in not being able to behave authentically causes us to *spell* it "anger." Further, the sadness of the loss of our playful nature causes us to *spell* it "grief."

Yet, these are just concepts—mental labels given to resisted energy within our emotional body. There is no such thing as fear, anger, or grief. There is just energy no longer in motion, which is causing heat, heat, and more heat.

Global warming.

‹ 6 ›

"*Nice* to See You All"

LET us return to our illustration, our dramatized timeline moving from childhood to adulthood. We now take a leap from the experience of the cool teenager to the aspiring young professional. We enter our experience as a young, hard working adult, just prior to *not* receiving that promotion.

As a young professional, we have been earning real money for the first time in our life. We have accordingly acquired an apartment and started buying stuff. It's no fun buying stuff if we have no one to show it to, so we invite some people from the office to come over and admire our purchases.

As the particular evening draws near, and our friends are about to arrive, we begin to feel jubilant. However, this rising feeling of joyfulness now appears to us as anxiety—as apprehension and nervousness. Anxiety is an interesting word; within it is the phrase, *any exit*.

If we have any connection at all to the child within us, we real eyes our heart longs to dance up and down the hallway of our new apartment chanting, "Here they come, my friends from work, coming to see my stuff! They are coming to see all my brand new stuff!"

However, we do not even real eyes we are jubilant. Instead, as our guests arrive and walk towards our apartment, we unconsciously associate this rising energetic state with the emotional signature imprinted during childhood when we were reprimanded for "misbehaving." We therefore draw upon the act that was acknowledged and appreciated back then. We coolly open our front door and say, "Good evening, nice to see you all, come on in and make yourselves comfortable."

Self-Medication

NOW that we are an adult, we have embraced appropriate and acceptable behaviors that we can rely on to sedate and camouflage our surfacing state of anxiety. The adult world has clearly modeled to us the means for reacting to our anxiety:

- If the jubilant energy attempts to rise up, we *sedate* it.

- If the jubilant energy arises and actually gets out of its box, we do whatever we can to *control* it.

The adult world has provided us with acceptable means for accomplishing sedation and control—alcohol and cigarettes. If anxiety arises and we want to sedate it, we can pour ourselves a drink. If this nervous energy gets out of hand and we do not know what is happening to us, we can light up a cigarette. Then, at least we know what is happening; we are having a cigarette. We are in control again. Sedating and controlling our emotional body is also called self-medication.

Other activities that may be used as self-medicating behaviors include eating, sex, work, talking, sleeping, watching TV, golf, working out, spiritual practices, attending support group meetings, religion, heroin, and politics. Self-medication includes any activity we consciously and unconsciously use to avoid feeling what we are feeling right now. These behaviors are passed like a baton through imprinting and example from one member of the human race to another.

Good Hospital

As our friends from the office enter our apartment, we invite them to have a drink and maybe to enjoy a cigarette. Because they are more than likely also feeling jubilant, but unable to express it—and this resistance within them is causing friction and the consequential buildup of heat—they appreciate our generous hospitality.

Soon, we gather around the table and eat food. This also helps add to our arsenal of avoidance and distraction. As the evening progresses, we continue to engage in whatever behaviors of sedation and control are required to make our time together a "nice" one—delicious desert, a coffee, a cigar, and a brandy. Providing the means for our visitors to self-medicate, to sedate and control their inner discomfort, is called "good *hospital*-ity."

If we have become one of *the cool crowd*, we may toke on a joint together. Marijuana is extremely efficient in calming anxiety because it combines both sedation and control. As far as tools of self-medication go, marijuana has few equals. Once we are stoned, we may convincingly discuss topics like peace on earth and matters of spiritual significance.

Because marijuana is so efficient at cutting off all authentic awareness of our emotional body condition, it allows us to actually believe we are peace-loving people. Because it artificially and temporarily opens our energy system and gives us a sense of movement and expansiveness without having to consciously integrate our emotional blockages, it allows us to feel as if we are having some sort of spiritual experience. However, it is all inauthentic. For those who only experience these states through its use, these states are *only* available through its use.

A "Normal" Adult

CONTINUAL self-medication in one form or another is our condition by the time we are a "normal" adult.

We have successfully sedated and controlled all awareness of our emotional body. We have completely departed the state of presence and fully embraced the state of pretence. We maintain this charade with our medicines and avoidance rituals.

The funny thing is, we have absolutely no idea that we are even in this condition. How can we? We have no in-sight into the causal aspect of our experience, and so we cannot perceive that we are completely out of integrity.

We are doing whatever we can just to appear as nice as possible, and to have as nice a time as is humanly possible.

Like everyone else, we are doing our best to excel in the pursuit of happiness.

Only other people appear to have a problem. We are not *addicted* or anything like that. Addiction is a sickness that only inflicts the weak, lost, and wayward citizens of skid row.

Really, we are not addicted. We are just having a social drink with our friends.

Addiction

THE reality of our situation is that if we are an adult living upon the earth as it is now, we have fully entered the experience of addiction.

We may tell ourselves that addicts are those broken people or losers who live on the other side of town, and that they are those people who have to go to weekly meetings. This is only because we too have entered denial by accepting the conveniently appropriate current perception of what addiction is.

Success and addiction are not bedfellows, the adult world tells us. So, as successful people, or people aspiring to be successful, we have to place the reality of addiction as far away from our current experience as possible.

Even if we are addicted to alcohol, cigarettes, or marijuana, we may still live within the delusion that when we overcome *these* obvious addictive behaviors, we will no longer be addicted. The story we may tell ourselves is that once we overcome these habits, we will once again be acceptable in our society.

However, when we take the steps to cleanse our life experience of these evident addictive traits, we invariably real eyes that these obvious surface behaviors are merely the tip of the addiction iceberg:

- We are addicted to saying "yes" when we mean "no," and "no" when we mean "yes."

- We are addicted to reacting—addicted to the fake and emotionally-driven acts we take out whenever we need to feel safe and accepted.

- We are addicted to being "nice."

- We are addicted to food, sex, and work.

- We are addicted to behaving as if the effect is the cause.

- We are addicted to behaving backwards.

Then there are even more subtle, hard-to-perceive addictions, like those we have to electricity and cooked food. If we enter an experience where there is absolutely no electricity for more than a few days, we start exhibiting the same withdrawal symptoms as any junkie going cold turkey. When we are deprived of electricity and cooked food, we start exhibiting cold and flu-like symptoms. Our thoughts become confused, and our emotional state becomes authentic.

The authentic condition of a normal adult emotional body is that it is riddled with suppressed fear, anger, and grief.

Addiction Is Inauthenticity

BY the time we are a normal adult, there is nothing we fear more than our authentic emotional state—our suppressed fear, anger, and grief. We say and do anything to sedate and control these out of our awareness.

Yet, what is an addiction? The phonetics of the word contain a revelation about this state, as well as the keys to our liberation from it. What is our "diction?" It is the way we speak—our way of verbally expressing ourselves.

When we are unable to speak our truth—unable to express ourselves authentically, in the moment we are required to—we *add* something to replace our inability to initiate authentic *diction*. This addition, whatever it is, becomes our addiction. Add + diction = addiction.

The moment we are able to express ourselves authentically is the moment we liberate ourselves from the trappings of this inauthentic experience. To accomplish this requires growing up emotionally. The moment we are able to emotionally lean upon ourselves, we no longer lean upon our crutches.

Any behavior we resort to in order to avoid feeling what we are really feeling in any given moment is an addiction. Any path we step upon that returns us to authenticity gradually liberates us from this spell.

Midlife Crisis

THERE was a time in our experience as a human species when, for most of our lives, we were able to suppress our awareness of our emotional body condition. This endeavor to live in a state of complete self-denial, keeping ourselves utterly sedated and controlled, is called "the pursuit of happiness."

Traditionally, for most of our human experience, we have been able to submerge our inner discomfort through the pursuit of happiness. Under these circumstances, it is only as we approach the moment of our death that the truth of our emotional condition begins surfacing—and hence our deep-seated fear of death.

Even in the midst of our relentless pursuit of happiness, the universe will at some point attempt to assist us by triggering an awareness of our inner turmoil. Traditionally this triggering event happens between the ages of forty and sixty. Suddenly, for no reason we can perceive, we will go through a shocking awakening as the authentic condition of our emotional body begins surfacing uncontrollably into our awareness.

As this occurs, we begin to real eyes that our entire life is inauthentic and not what we truly want after all. Rather, it is a pretentious mask that we wear to hide what we are afraid of—an artificial act to attract the acknowledgement we feel we didn't receive from our parents.

This surfacing awareness arises from within our emotional body, and is in fact the emotional body attempting to liberate itself from its energetic incarceration. Because the age of our emotional body was stunted at somewhere between the ages of seven and fourteen, we reacted to this arising awareness immaturely—such as by buying a red sports car, finding a younger model of our marriage partner to sit in the passenger seat, and driving off into the sunset.

This sudden awareness of our emotional body's true condition erupting within the midst of our relentless pursuit of happiness is traditionally known as a midlife crisis.

Symptom

WE no longer have the luxury of waiting for a midlife crisis to bring our attention to the unintegrated condition of our emotional body. Life upon earth as we experience it right now *is* a midlife crisis.

Our collectively unfolding midlife crisis is now evident as the ever-widening appearance of deeply uncomfortable human symptoms.

The word symptom is phonetically self-descriptive; it reads "some time." A symptom is the outer evidence of an inner time-based experience (some time) that is unintegrated to the point that the energetic expression of our emotional turmoil is exhibited externally through mental confusion and physical discomfort.

Everything from cancer to crime, from social conflict to mental instability, from broken relationships to pretentious spiritual behavior, from drug addiction to infatuation with technology is a symptom reflecting emotional body imbalance. Symptoms show us through *out-sight* what it is we are no longer able to perceive through *in-sight*. All mental and physical symptoms that commence after birth are outer manifestations of an emotional body in crisis.

We have now arrived at the point on the timeline of our illustrative dramatization at which we have fully entered the world of the adult. Our life experience is a symptom. There are millions and millions just like us, living with absolutely no awareness of their emotional body condition, and their lives are a symptom of this lack of awareness. And, to whom do we turn for assistance? When we fail in our personal attempts at self-medication, we invariably seek out the assistance of another, especially those who either have degrees hanging on walls or wild imaginations. Thus we become exposed to their tried and tested self-medicating behaviors, whether these are pharmaceuticals or New Age philosophies.

One of the highest causes of death in the USA is medical treatment. This is because the health practitioners we go to are just as unaware of their own emotional body condition as we are. Consequently, they can only react to our pleas for assistance in the same manner that they sedate and control themselves.

‹ 7 ›

Time-Based Paradigm

WHEN we first hear about the state of being called present moment awareness, we attempt to initiate it by making physical adjustments to our life experience.

Because our attention is trance fixed by the physical aspect of our experience, we assume that something outside of us, like clock time, is the culprit that has led us into the perceptual imprisonment of living in a time-based paradigm. So, we take off our watches in order to be "in the moment" and not be dictated to by the time of day.

This is a misunderstanding. It is not a clock but the unintegrated experiences imprinted within our emotional body in the first seven years of our life that drag us into a time-based paradigm.

Driven by the intent to figure out what happened and to try to stop whatever it was that happened from happening again, these initial moments of unintegrated time unconsciously tug upon our attention. Trying to figure out what happened engages us in a perceptual paradigm that becomes our *past*. Trying to figure out how to stop whatever happened from happening again engages us in a perceptual paradigm that becomes our *potential future*.

This ongoing behavior, which is steered from within the causal point of the quality of our life experience, the emotional body, is the hook that holds us within the perceptual experience we call a time-based paradigm. This hook is also known in Shamanic circles as "the assemblage point."

Physically Anchored Awareness

BY the time we are adults, we all exhibit symptoms of being mentally confined within a time-based paradigm. How we interact with these symptoms reveals our state of awareness.

To demon straight this, let us examine an extreme example such as being diagnosed with a terminal illness like cancer. When our awareness is anchored primarily in the physical, so that we are completely physically trance fixed by our experience, our approach to such a diagnosis is entirely physically-based. We attempt to have our physical body sedated, controlled, cut, nuked, and drugged. From within this perceptual paradigm, we behave as if removing all physical evidence of the disease from our awareness cures the condition.

Accidents, addictions, and diseases form a trinity of consequences resulting from unconscious behaviors that emanate from our collective, unintegrated emotional body condition.

If medical doctors really had the capacity to eliminate the roots of accidents, addictions, and diseases, we would only need a few of them on the planet and hardly anyone would require their services.

Mentally Anchored Awareness

WHEN our awareness becomes slightly more expanded, we may attract to ourselves a physician who, after diagnosing us as having cancer, says, "You may want to talk to someone about this."

This approach arises from the awareness that our physical state is somehow connected with our mental state.

In taking this guidance, we may choose to see a therapist. However, if we believe for a moment that talking can make any real and lasting adjustment to the quality of our experience, we may wish to discover why the word therapist spells out the words "the rapist."

If talking accomplished anything real, the earth's population would be at peace by now and everyone would be happy and healthy.

When we are paying money to talk to someone, we have to make sure we have something significant to say. We have to have a good story. The more we sit and tell someone what we *think* about what happened to us, and what this means to us, the more stories we are telling. We become the snake eating its tail.

These stories are all mental interpretations of an emotional condition, and any mental interpretation of an emotional condition is the doorway to complete misinterpretation.

When someone we are paying, who is qualified after years of book study and has impressive certificates on the wall, affirms the reality of our stories, we have cause to believe them to be true—even if we made them up! The moment we believe these stories, we are perceptually imprisoned by them.

If traditional therapy had the capacity to alter the causal point of the quality of our experience, no one would be sitting in front of a therapist for years and years without any end in sight.

Visiting a therapist to seek relief is the addiction of a mental culture.

A Bad Rap

DOCTORS and traditional therapists get a bad rap because we go to them for all the wrong reasons. It is our intent, when entering their services, that makes it impossible for them to do what they are trained for.

A medical doctor is the master of physical trauma, while a traditional therapist is the master of mental construct. However, neither physical trauma nor mental construct are causal. They are symptoms, effects. Medical doctors and traditional therapists are able to sedate and control effects, not adjust causes.

If we are hit by a car, it is not helpful to be taken to a Reiki master, an aroma therapist, or an acupuncturist. We must be taken to a doctor. A doctor knows how to mend the physical aspects of our body's trauma.

However, if we have terminal cancer, and our symptoms have not yet reached a point where we are about to lose our physical body, it is clearly unwise to expect a doctor to "cure" us. Doctors have proven that they can diagnose cancer, just as they have proven they cannot cure it. If they had the capacity to cure it, why do people still have this illness?

Also, unless we specifically request counseling to calm and clarify our mental processes, we ought not go near a traditional therapist if we have been diagnosed with a terminal condition. If talking about disease or our experience of it had any real impact on our condition, the human family would be in supreme health by now.

Ignorance Peddles Drugs

IF we go to someone who does not have the capacity to make an authentic adjustment to the causal point of our experience, because of their arrogance they also do not have the capacity to tell us the truth— that they do not have a clue what to do!

Instead, they do what everyone else is doing, what they have been taught to do, or what they are currently doing to themselves. Both doctors and medically trained therapists, when faced with their inherent limitations, react instinctively by prescribing pharmaceuticals.

Pharmaceuticals kill more people than illegal street drugs. Not only this, but by starting on one course of pharmaceuticals, one often has to take additional medication in an attempt to contain the side-effects triggered by the initial treatment.

Pharmaceuticals are efficient in sedating and controlling symptoms, which is sometimes necessary, but they are *in-effect-you-all* in adjusting the causal point of an imbalanced human experience. Pharmaceuticals are not a cure.

When used instead of self-examination, pharmaceuticals cover up our awareness of the authentic condition of the emotional body. In this light, they are an addiction.

We must call pharmaceuticals what they are—they are drugs.

Everyone who takes these drugs without intending to adjust the causal point of their condition through self-examination is an addict using these substances for sedation and control.

Unless we look straight into the face of this miserable human condition and see it for what it is, we are unable to face it. The more ignorant a medical practitioner is, the more pharmaceuticals they prescribe.

Checking Out or Checking In

WHEN our awareness becomes still more expanded, we may attract to us a physician who not only recommends that we speak to someone, because this may definitely be useful, but who also asks us, "What is going on with you emotionally?"

Underlying all uncomfortable physical symptoms and states of mental confusion is *an emotional signature.*

There are physicians and traditional therapists who are now awakening to the reality that unless this emotional signature is integrated, no amount of talking and physical manipulation of our dis-ease will impact the quality of our experience in any authentic manner.

When we have entered severe symptomatic discomfort, whether we reach this point of awareness determines whether we begin to "check out" or begin "checking in."

Checking out is behavior born of a victim and victor mentality. It assumes our life experience is happening to us, and that to survive it we must overcome it. From this frame of reference, the symptom is an enemy coming to hurt us that must be snuffed out at all cost.

Checking in perceives our physical symptoms and mental confusion as allies that have come to show us where we are already hurting— allies that must be listened to attentively with the eyes of our heart.

Once we make this connection, our journey into authenticity is in full stride. Accordingly, we no longer moan about the company we are keeping or about the food we are eating. Nor do we enter into blame by shouting at the waiter for the quality of the food on the table. We real eyes the waiter does not cook the food—we do.

We real eyes there is a kitchen and that we have a say in what happens in the kitchen. We real eyes that the kitchen is to be found *in the heart* through awakening our felt-perception. It is at this point in our journey that we gracefully excuse ourselves from the table and seek out the kitchen to enter the heady experience of cooking. It is at this point that we surrender to an initiation into integrity.

Fix Me

OTHERS can do physical activities for us. They can also move physical things around on our behalf. If they are strong enough, they can even pick us up and carry us around. Because of this, if we are trance fixed by the physical, we are likely to believe that another's physical behavior or presence can change the quality of our experience for us in a real and lasting way.

This assumption opens the door to a victim and victor mentality. When we are in discomfort, being physically trance fixed causes us to seek outside ourselves for someone or something to "fix us" through physical impact. This perceptual error and the behavior it initiates causes many of us to enter experiences that result in checking out.

Others can also perform mental activities for us. They can discuss our affairs on our behalf. They can stand up in a court of law and verbally represent us. Because of this, if we are trance fixed by the mental, we are likely to believe that the words or thoughts of another can somehow change the quality of our experience for us in a real and lasting way.

This assumption also opens the door to a victim and victor mentality.

When we are in discomfort, being mentally trance fixed causes us to seek outside of ourselves for someone else to "fix us" through talking, analysis, and understanding. This perceptual error and the behavior it initiates also causes many of us to enter experiences that result in checking out.

Empowerment

No one can *feel* for us. No one can feel on our behalf. We cannot approach another and say, "I am going to take this week off. Won't you feel for me until I get back?" We must feel for ourselves.

We are each completely responsible for our feelings *because* no one can feel for us. Consequently, we are completely responsible for the condition of our emotional body. *Our heart is our responsibility*. Only the emotionally immature place the responsibility of their heart in the hands of another.

When, by integrating the consequences of The Pathway of Awareness, we real eyes that the causal point of the quality of our experience is determined by the condition of our emotional body—and that only we have the capacity to feel what this is, and therefore to adjust it— then we are empowered in the real sense of the word.

Until the moment we real eyes this, we live backwards, pacing in circles within the confines of an invisible perceptual prison.

Once we real eyes this, we may still require information on how to make adjustments to the present condition of our emotional body. But from this moment on we are at least aware that no one else can really know what is actually happening to us, or within us, the way we do.

In this moment, we also real eyes that whatever has to be initiated to restore balance to our experience must be initiated by ourselves. Realizing this, accepting this, and committing to take full responsibility for this aspect of our human experience is the precise moment we are able to embrace whatever it takes to check in.

The moment we begin consciously checking in is the precise moment we start drastically decreasing the possibility of unconsciously checking out. This is when the expression, "Whatever it takes, for heaven's sake," takes on a whole new meaning. This is when we take our first step towards initiating a conversation with the unspeakable.

By accepting responsibility for the causal point of our experience, we enter the journey of authentic self-empowerment. We are empowering ourselves to consciously approach an encounter with "the self"—to enter a conversation with the unspeakable.

The moment we consciously choose to impact the causal point of our experience is also the moment our outer experience ceases to be something that is *happening to us*. It reveals itself as an experience that is *happening through us*—and in this light, it no longer "matters" as much.

Our Plight

WE are now reaching completion of our exploration into the experience of the physically transfixed human being. We have arrived at the perceptual juncture called "the adult."

This is a way of existing in which we are partially perceptually blind, habitually reactive and inauthentic, and stumble through life deeply unconscious about the causal point of our predicament—the condition of our interior. For the most part we have absolutely no idea that this is our plight.

To live this way appears normal when everyone behaves accordingly. Most of us remain in this dazed and confused state for the rest of our days, existing in quiet desperation, doing the best we can with the limited level of awareness we have. This has been the fate of the countless generations before us.

We have tried to escape our suffering with our tools and technology by imposing our will on the physical aspect of our experience. We have tried to escape our suffering through our thinking by trying to "understand what happened," and by developing psychological models and spiritual systems that are intended to liberate us. Yet, we have failed to liberate humanity because we cannot escape the consequences of unconscious behavior through sedation and control of the mental and physical aspects of our human experience. We cannot impact the causal point of our suffering by tampering with its effects. Attempting to do so is insanity.

How does a species that has gone completely mad collectively navigate itself into sanity? Maybe the answer has nothing to do with doing anything *together*.

Unattended Interior

TRADITIONALLY, as physically trance fixed humans, our entire life experience has been unconsciously driven by seeking shade from the heat of our inner emotional turmoil. This is the reason for our relentless pursuit of happiness.

We may not be happy now, but the promise of the adult world is that one day we will be. For the most part, we believe this tired old story—this dream of eventual success and relief—because society shuns the telling of any other story.

We cling to familiarity, even if the familiar is almost unbearable.

Our collective mentality turns on anyone who attempts to liberate us from our collective spellbinding dream by awakening us to the possibility of individually exploring a vision of our interior. We turn on such individuals by subjecting them to conceptual analysis, and sometimes by simply physically murdering them. We also turn on them with emotionally-driven superstitious worship, which is a state of child(ish)-like belief in a power outside ourselves that will "get us" if we don't believe what everyone else believes. Such a belief is driven unconsciously by the unintegrated (undeveloped, traumatized, immature) condition of the emotional body. It is to believe such things as, "If you do not accept Jesus as your savior, the boogyman will get you!"

There is nothing more threatening to a human being than the possibility of authentic liberation from what has "always been so." We want change *as long as everything stays the same.*

Retirement

MOST of us plow through life robotically until a stage called "retirement," at which point we hand the baton of despair over to the younger generation. During our lifetime's toil, few of us establish enough resources to decay comfortably into old age, and so most of us decay in despair.

Once retirement is reached and the constant unending activity of life is minimized or removed, our ability to suppress the authentic condition of our emotional body quickly weakens and diminishes. Accordingly, our latter years are plagued with an increasing array of physical ailments, states of mental confusion, and emotional turmoil—symptomatic reflections of the unattended condition of our immature emotional body.

For many of us this leads to increased doses of medication, whether self-administered or through pharmaceutical prescription. Many of our elders today spend more of their precious resources on medications than on food.

This culmination of desperation and decay experienced during the "old age" part of our human experience is a testament to a life lived without conscious exploration into the condition of the interior.

What makes this predicament so pitiful is that we assume this deterioration is normal—that this is our fate.

Going In

WHAT makes being alive today different from any recent era is that we are no longer condemned to this fate of decaying miserably into old age. We have, as a species, gathered enough collective awareness so that this plight may be effectively altered by the individual.

We no longer have to face our latter years in fear and doubt, in deep discomfort and despair. We now have the option to take "the heart of the matter" into our own hands. We can take responsibility for the causal point of the quality of our human experience by consciously tending to the condition of our emotional body. This is the promise of this generation. This is the hope of the world. This is the heart of the matter.

Knowing we can impact our lives in such a way as to transform our latter years into a healthy and conscious moment of transition from this earthly experience into the next is in many ways a return to the quality of *beingness* last experienced when we were in touch with our indigenous nature.

Yet, this is not about *a going back* to that era, as in stepping into the past. This is *a going in*, as in stepping into the resonance of the immense possibilities of this moment.

‹ 8 ›

The Turning Point

THIS seemingly terrifying moment in which our species appears to be floundering on the edge of a chaotic abyss is the turning point. We are in the midst of a planetary rite of passage, which is inviting us into the authentic embrace of personal responsibility.

The gift within this invitation is a relationship with life reborn— a way of being on earth so unfamiliar to us that trying to communicate it is as fragile as drawing a line across the surface of a pool of water.

Our current nightmare is our planetary experience of being in the midst of a vision quest that is being overseen by the unseen elders of our human destiny.

As a species, we have trodden our way wearily through the world of manufacturing and have now arrived at the doorway to the consciousness of creativity. Whereas *manufacture* is the art of manipulating and adjusting the exterior, *creativity* is the art of mastering the interior.

At this new frontier, manufacture is ineffectual. Within the unfolding paradigm of authentic creativity, a collective impact on our experience can only be accomplished through the integrity of precisely focused individual activity—through the diamond integrity of personal responsibility.

Our current confusion arises out of standing with one foot in each of these worlds. We are still trying to do mentally and physically what only the heart can accomplish. We are still trying to *do collectively* what can only *be accomplished individually*.

We are still *trying to feel better,* when we are now being asked to *get better at feeling*.

Though it may appear complicated to the mental body, it only takes one conscious and deliberate step to pass through this portal in order to take the evolutionary leap toward which our entire species is now being thrust.

Stepping consciously through this portal is the heart of the matter. It requires felt-perception.

Clarifying Our Intent

THE turning point in our individual experience that authentically impacts the collective condition of our species is when we deliberately explore our interior condition, familiarizing ourselves with the authentic state of our emotional body.

It is only by consciously bringing awareness to the causal point of the quality of our experience that we impact its condition, and consequently transform the entire resonance of our human experience.

The highest intent for embarking on such a quest is not—as our political, economic and religious systems lead us to believe—to free humanity of suffering. Rather, it is to free ourselves from our perceptual imprisonment by entering an experiential conversation with the unspeakable. By individually setting an example of what is possible through the parameters of our personal experience, we open a portal of possibility within the common experience. This portal is available to all who are ready to initiate perceptual liberation, without interfering with anyone else's current experience.

Trying to "save the world" is an unintegrated, reactive condition—an outwardly projected symptom of *a helpless person trying to stamp out the reflection of their own helplessness in the world by helping others*.

"Saving" anyone is arrogant interference. There is nothing noble in trying to save others from having their own experience. Only more ills are born of such missionary madness.

Authentic liberation arises only from "doing unto ourselves as we would have others do unto us." Wanting others to behave like us and to believe in what we believe is not liberation—it is camouflaged judgment.

Evolution is encouraged through example, not conversion.

Reversing the Pathway

To initiate our quest to enter a conversation with the unspeakable, we systematically retrace our steps along The Pathway of Awareness, consciously making a shift from externalization to internalization.

Consciously reversing The Pathway of Awareness is the key to deprogramming ourselves from our current state of perceptual incarceration. It gradually awakens us from the spell of unconscious reactive behavior into the responsive and self-empowered resonance of operating out of present moment awareness.

Before we map out the terrain for this next leg of our adventure, it is useful to briefly review The Pathway of Awareness by way of examining its ongoing play within the mundane activities of our daily life experience. This review empowers us to perceive how we are routinely, and for the most part unconsciously, moving along this pathway from emotional to mental to physical in practically every activity of our life experience.

Bringing as much awareness as is possible to this unconscious condition is useful when it is our intention to reverse our relationship with it. Reversing our relationship with The Pathway of Awareness goes against the grain of the ancient tide of humanity's perception of what life is about. It transforms us into *upstream swimmers*.

Within the flow of this text, our brief review of The Pathway of Awareness is our final approach to the turning point, from unconsciously checking out to consciously checking in.

The Stuff of Life

THIS brief recap of the natural flow of our awareness in manifesting our daily human experience is most easily accomplished by examining one of our favorite pastimes— buying "stuff."

We humans like buying stuff and behave as if we believe the purchase of stuff can make us forever happy. We work very hard to earn money to buy lots of stuff, and live in a perceptual mind-set in which one cannot possibly have enough stuff—especially the "latest" stuff. Our relationship with stuff is therefore an appropriate one in which to witness The Pathway of Awareness in play.

Why I Want It

FOR the sake of illustration, let us observe a woman who sees a dress she wants. If she is trance fixed by the physical, she may tell herself she wants this dress because it is beautifully designed or because the fabric is so exquisite. If she is more mentally trance fixed, she may tell herself she wants this particular dress because the distinct designer label guarantees a product of the highest quality.

Yet, neither the physical nor mental aspect of this shopping encounter is the causal momentum that is driving the desire for this particular dress.

If the woman's emotional body awareness were awakened, she would real eyes that what initially attracts her to the dress is the promise of a feeling. She unconsciously believes that if she purchases this garment and wears it, she will *feel* good, happy, sexy, admired, wealthy, and successful.

The intended *feeling* is the causal point of her attraction to the garment, and the desire for this intended feeling is driven by the current condition of her emotional body.

The Pathway of Manifestation

ONCE the woman in our illustration believes the dress can enable her to achieve her intent to manifest a desired emotional state, she moves obediently along The Pathway of Awareness.

Next, she mentally visits the possibility of obtaining the item. She asks herself questions such as: How much does it cost? Can I afford this? Does the asking price of this dress equal the enjoyment I intend to have by wearing it? Do I pay cash or put it on my credit card? How long will it take me to pay this off? By purchasing this dress, what do I have to go without that I may have otherwise used the money on?

As the woman goes through these calculations, the mental body serves as the corridor that delivers her from *desiring the intended feeling,* towards *physically acquiring the item* that makes the experience possible.

Once the mental body has made all the necessary calculations, if the feeling is still desired and perceived to be worth the expenditure, the dress is physically purchased, taken home, and worn.

The woman's experience has moved from emotional to mental to physical.

The Causal Point

ONCE the transaction is complete and the woman is now wearing the garment, the emotional body remains the causal point of the intended experience. This is evident from the power of the feedback she receives while wearing it.

If her friends give her *that look*—the one that says, "No honey, that dress does *not* look good on you"—or if during the course of the evening anything happens that causes her to *feel* uncomfortable about wearing it—that's it. It's all over. She never wears that dress again.

No matter how much she paid for it, and no matter which designer created it, if she *feels* uncomfortable in it, or about it, that dress might as well be thrown into the trash. Why? Because *the feeling aspect of her experience is the causal point.*

This movement along The Pathway of Awareness also applies to men buying trucks, children receiving toys, and all the stuff we accumulate to keep up with the Jones'.

It also applies to anything we purchase to stuff down our inner discomfort, or in an attempt to feed ourselves outwardly and unconsciously with superficially generated emotional resonances that we are not yet mature enough to consciously activate within ourselves.

The Shallow Outer

IT isn't even necessary for us to feel uncomfortable about the stuff we have purchased for us to lose interest in it. We may purchase stuff that initially facilitates us into feeling really good, but because this feeling is generated by outside influences and not by inner emotional capacities, the feeling inevitably decays.

The moment the intensity of a feeling associated with any item, activity, or experience decays beyond a certain point, we let go of our attachment to and association with it. Why? Because *the feeling aspect of our experience is the causal point of our attachment to anything.*

No feeling, no attachment. It is that simple and that powerful.

And, we may be grateful that this is so, because we now have a clue as to where we have to direct our awareness in order to take full responsibility for the causal point of the quality—the felt content—of our life experience.

Accordingly, we may now begin moving efficiently inward upon a journey into perceptual integrity.

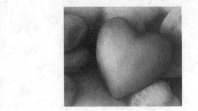

‹ 9 ›

Having An Experience

E NTERING a conversation with the unspeakable does not require learning something new. It is an act of remembrance.

The word "remember" phonetically tells us what this entails. To re-member is to become a member again. A member of what? The whole. Entering a conversation with the unspeakable is about re-identifying with that which is already whole.

All through this text, we have been discussing the origins of entering a behavior that is backwards. We have been realizing how we have come to mistakenly perceive the effect as being the cause.

One of the consequences of this behavior is that we have become identified with our outer physical experience to the point that we now seek ourselves within this outer experience, and consequently lose an awareness of ourselves within it.

For example, we no longer see an addictive state as *an experience we are having,* but as *something we have become.* We now perceive ourselves as an addict. Instead of realizing that we are having an experience of alcohol addiction, we perceptually incarcerate ourselves within the experience by erroneously declaring, "I *am* an alcoholic."

We enter a conversation with the unspeakable when we real eyes *we are not the experience we are having.* Rather, *we are having an experience.*

What Is Reading This Page?

LET me, as the writer of this text, address you directly for a moment. Who is reading the text in front of you right now?

You may reply, "I am."

It is easy for you to perceptually step back from the act of reading this text and identify yourself as the one having the experience of reading. It is clear to you that you are not the physical book in your hands. It is also clear to you that you are not the conceptual material contained in the text on the page in front of you. Neither are you the emotional responses generated by the act of reading this text. It is clear that you are having an experience of reading the text of this book.

So who, or more precisely, *what* is having this experience of reading this text?

Stop for a moment and sit with the sense of you not being the experience you are having right now, but rather of you being a witness to an experience that is unfolding right now.

Disentanglement

THE experience you are having right now is limited by its physical, mental, and emotional parameters, whereas whatever *you* are is not.

You can put this book down and exchange this experience for another as readily as you can choose to continue having this experience. You are not bound by this reading experience. Why, then, do you assume that you are bound by *any* experience in your life to the point that it appears to possess you beyond your personal will?

Why is it easy to put this book down? Go ahead and do it. Play along with me here for a moment and put this book down for a few seconds. Then pick it up again. You see how easy it is.

Why is it that you have complete control over this reading experience, but not over other experiences in your life?

If you were *not* able to put this book down when asked, would you then helplessly declare, "I am a reader?" Of course not. Yet, when we are addicted to an experience we cannot appear to assert our will over, like drinking alcohol, we automatically make statements such as, "I am an alcoholic."

This is the same as declaring, when we have to go to the restroom, "I am a urinater" as opposed to "I am having an experience of urinating."

Holy

WHENEVER we identify with an experience by declaring "I *am* this" or "I *am* that," we are weaving a hypnotic *spell* into a perceptual *sentence* and then believing *our story*.

Despite all the stories we tell ourselves about who and what we are, there is a part of us that is able to step out of any experience we are currently having as a "witness" or "observer." This part of us is always whole and untouched by any physical, mental, or emotional experience.

The more we identify with this whole part of ourselves, the more integrated, or whole, we feel. This part of us is holy.

"Holiness" is a word that is physically misrepresented, mentally corrupted, and emotionally charged by religious indoctrination. Holiness is simply wholeness.

We automatically enter a conversation with the unspeakable when we embrace our wholeness. Such an encounter is holy.

Taking Charge

THE root cause of our schizophrenic condition—in which we are sometimes aware we are *having* an experience, and then at other times are completely unconscious and imagine we are being *possessed* by an experience—lies in the condition of our emotional body.

When our emotional body is not in balance, we do not experience ourselves as whole. Instead, we project our attention outward into whatever experience we mistakenly believe will make us whole.

Being possessed by an experience, and hence appearing to be addicted to it, is the consequence of being unconsciously driven by a *charge*. This charge is an emotional signature that for the most part remains hidden from us and therefore drives our experience unconsciously.

We know this is true, because the moment we attempt to extricate ourselves from any experience we perceive ourselves to be addicted to—any experience with which we have completely identified— we begin to *feel* awful. It is to sedate and control this emerging awful feeling that we re-enter the state of "possession." It is to sedate and control this awful feeling that we entered the behavior that grew into an addictive encounter in the first place.

Being aware that we are having an experience—one which we can pick up and put down as effortlessly as we can this book—is to real eyes that *we are in charge*. But we are only in charge when we are consciously taking charge of the causal point of the quality of our experience, when we accept full responsibility for the condition of our emotional body, and when we are at peace with *all our feelings*.

We only become *the author* of our experience when we consciously attend to its *emotional signature*. Until we reach this point, the unintegrated experience of an imprinted seven-year-old takes the reins on our behalf.

To be an adult driven by the unintegrated condition of a child is to be out of integrity.

Praying for Help

MANY of us, whether we admit it or not, real eyes it or not, pray for help. We pray for help because we have become possessed by an uncomfortable experience and seek assistance in being released. This experience may appear in our circumstances as addiction, lack, disease, heartbreak, or any variety of manifestations of physical, mental, and emotional distress.

When we pray, we are asking assistance from the vibrational, although we may not perceive that this is what we are doing. We may say that we are speaking to God, or calling upon Jesus, or begging for the mercy of Mohammed, or requesting a blessing of the Buddha, or calling upon The Great Spirit.

It does not matter how we describe our intent. What is profound is that we all tread The Pathway of Awareness in exactly the same manner when we seek assistance from a higher power. We reverse it.

Reversing the Pathway

ALL religions—and this includes indigenous cultures—when intending to speak to what God is for them, or to any of God's representa-
tives, reverse The Pathway of Awareness.

First, they adopt a physical posture or make other physical prepa-
rations. This may involve putting their hands together in a prayer position, going down on their knees, falling face down to the earth, lighting
incense, sitting in a lotus position, lighting a ceremonial fire, throwing
herbs on coals, drinking and eating a sacramental substance, entering
a physical temple or church, traveling to a sacred physical location,
wearing holy garments, or holding a power symbol or sacred object.

The physical practice or preparation is then followed by a mental
activity. This may be speaking a prayer, reading from a holy book,
chanting a mantra, singing a hymn, or engaging in some other manner
of conveying a mental message or conceptualized request.

The initiation of physical arrangements and mental communications is intended to activate an experience. This experience is initially
grounded in the emotional body as the emergence of a particular
feeling.

If the feeling is not present, or does not at some point arise as a consequence of the physical and mental efforts employed, the entire ritual
proves to be empty and inefficient. If the particular intended feeling
is present, it is accepted by all participants that the ritual has been
successful.

Taking Shortcuts

IN a shared experience like praying, we see that all of our human family, when approaching what God is for us, automatically reverse The Pathway of Awareness. We move along it from physical to mental to emotional.

To succeed with our intent to enter an awareness of our authentic essence beyond and above the transience of the physical, mental, and emotional currents of our daily life, we must deliberately reverse The Pathway of Awareness.

How do we enter an experiential conversation with the unspeakable—with the vibrational, which is a state of being beyond any of our transient doings? We must enter a journey as deliberate as the one our awareness traveled upon when entering our experience of life on earth.

When we do not real eyes this, we are likely to go astray. We may mistakenly attempt to take what looks like a shortcut. The desire to take shortcuts when approaching the vibrational is usually born out of desperation—out of the hope of immediately stilling our inner emotional discomfort.

Unfortunately, such an approach, which usually involves seeking to be fixed by another, opens us to deception. Seeking shortcuts makes us vulnerable to believing that if we offer our allegiance to another, whether an individual or an organization, the necessary steps into vibrational awareness can be taken by them on our behalf. Believing this is the same as believing that another can *feel* on our behalf.

Once we are aware of the steps we are required to take in approaching a conversation with the unspeakable—that we are to move our awareness consciously from the physical, through the mental, and into the emotional—we are well-equipped for the noblest adventure any human may intend. We are ready to journey with discernment and tread the pathway with integrity.

<‹ I O ›>

Living in the Mental

THE gift of conversing with the unspeakable is received *through* the flesh, not by denying it. The first step in entering a conversation with the unspeakable is therefore to "get into the body."

When we live in a time-based paradigm, we do not reside in our physical body. In fact, many of our behaviors are motivated by a desire to get out of our physical body. Getting out of it is a reaction to our ongoing anxiety—a word containing the phrase "any exit." All behaviors of sedation and control are intended to assist us to depart the physical by scampering into the mental.

We may assume we live within the physical body because it dutifully tags along everywhere with us, yet this is not so. In any given moment, we are wherever our attention is focused. How many times have we driven a car somewhere, and upon arriving at our destination, had no clear recall of how we got there?

Most of us function in this disembodied manner throughout much of our waking state. We spend much of our life experience in the mental realm, talking to ourselves, having mock conversations with others, thinking about what we have to do, how we are going to do it, when we are going to do it, and why we are going to do it. For the most part, we are oblivious of the only moment in which it is possible to accomplish anything—the *now!* The only place in which life is actively unfolding is in the present moment.

The fact that there are not cars piled up on every street corner is a clear testament to the existence of a presence called God. For the most part, we are not driving our life experiences; they are on autopilot. If there wasn't a divinely patient and compassionate presence taking the wheel as we stumble distractedly along the endless illusionary corridors of the mental plane, few of us would make it through a single day.

Into the Body

THE first step in "showing up" in the present moment, which is the domain of the vibrational, is therefore to re-enter and begin anchoring our awareness in the physical body.

To initiate physical presence is one of the great benefits of having a physical body, for it only exists in the present moment! By consciously entering it, we simultaneously bring our awareness into the present moment.

Not only is the physical body anchored in the present moment, it contains a precise record of whatever past experiences we have as yet not integrated. These records are available as physical "symptoms," or as the word phonetically suggests, as "some times"—as physical manifestations of moments in time that are unintegrated. The discomfort caused by these unintegrated moments is the causal momentum for our anxiety. It is the causal momentum for our constant attempt to find any exit from this moment, and therefore for our addiction to escaping from what we are feeling and getting into our thoughts.

By agreeing to consciously enter into our physical body, we make accessible to ourselves the awareness of why we are addicted to habitually fleeing from this moment.

Peace of Mind

DURING our journey together through this text, we have discussed the various attributes that come together to manufacture our human experience—the physical, mental, and emotional bodies. We have also deliberately minimized our use of the word "mind."

The mind, within the framework of this discussion, is the matrix in which we have our life experience, and also the means by which this experience is encountered. This is why it is accurate to claim that when we do not mind, it does not matter.

The trinity of this mind-matrix comprises the physical, mental, and emotional bodies. These three together are the mind as a whole. When these three attributes function with the resonance of integrity, the mind is holy.

We, *the one having the experience*—an experience we encounter through sensation, thought, feeling, and intuition—are vibrational. Whereas everything about the mind is constantly in a state of change, who we truly are cannot be altered. Only when we rest consciously within *the peace that we are* is the mind calmed.

Just as we seek self-awareness through consciously reawakening to our vibrational essence, so the mind seeks wholeness through physical, mental, and emotional integration. Only when all three of its attributes are integrated is the mind able to rest in peace. Remembering ourselves as vibrational is the catalyst for this level of integration. Until this remembrance takes place, the mind is like a fly buzzing around our hot sweaty face on a long summer's day.

Birthing Our Unconscious

DURING our first seven years of our life upon earth, we encounter a constant string of experiences called our "childhood." It is impossible for the mind to integrate these initial experiences because during these first seven years, we are primarily immersed in emotional body awareness.

We have not yet developed the capacity of conceptualization and therefore cannot integrate anything mentally. Neither have we gone through the necessary events and circumstances that provide an adequate container for physical integration. For this reason, what happens to us in childhood remains unintegrated and frozen in time.

The mind automatically seeks integration and therefore cannot rest within this predicament. It festers around each unintegrated moment of our childhood. This festering behavior sucks on our available attention and anchors it into these points of unintegrated time.

This festering is primarily energetic, and so as our emotional body awareness decays after childhood, this ongoing energetic condition becomes invisible to us. It becomes the activity of our unconsciousness.

Original Sin

BY the time we are adults, the mind—in its desire to achieve whole-ness—has recruited a vast amount of our available attention as an ac-complice in its desperate attempt to integrate what happened in the first seven years of our life experience.

The perceptual error we make is assuming that the mind's quest for wholeness is our true quest. By identifying with this ongoing energetic activity and unconsciously embracing it as ours, we enter a perceptual paradigm in which we believe we are no longer whole and must do something to reclaim the state of wholeness.

This perceptual error leaves us feeling broken and seeking to be fixed. By the time we enter the adult worldview, we are so bound by this experience of feeling broken that we have jumped ship from vibrational awareness and completely identified with our physical, mental, and emotional attributes.

This sense of brokenness—of identifying with a need to be fixed— is the source of our misplaced religious concepts of "original sin." A more appropriate word for sin is "dysfunction." Original sin is the dysfunctional patterns imprinted within our emotional body that unconsciously drive us into self-destructive behavior. These imprinted energetic patterns are the generational dysfunction passed along line-ages from parent to child. These must be neutralized if we are to re-enter an experiential awareness of our authentic vibrational essence.

Whenever we say, "I am a sinner," we are identifying with an unintegrated experience within the matrix of mind. This causes us to lose awareness of our authentic, unchanging, vibrational essence, which is passing through this experience.

By identifying with an emotionally charged experience like sin, we automatically shut off an awareness of what we really are, what God is for us, and where we truly reside right now. Those who teach that we *are* sinners mask the presence of Truth.

Parenting Mind

THE quest of entering a conversation with the unspeakable is not about fixing anything. It is about remembering something.

There is nothing to do to become whole. Being whole is our authentic state—one that knows no change. We have never been broken, nor can we accomplish brokenness. However, until we address the unintegrated condition of the mind, and participate *consciously* in its quest for its integration, we unconsciously get dragged into what it *thinks* it needs to do to find, make, or enforce peace.

Our task is to become the parental facilitator within this predicament by compassionately assisting the mind to integrate those childhood experiences that are the root of why so much of our attention is unconsciously sucked out of the present moment. As we empower the mind to integrate these childhood experiences, the aspects of our awareness that have mistakenly become an accomplice in this desperate quest automatically detach from these energetic entanglements and return to the present moment. The more they do, the more presence we *feel*.

Through consciously and consistently facilitating the integration of mind, we eventually regain enough presence to tangibly *feel* the essence of our vibrational identity in all its magnificence. Once we consciously initiate the mind's integrative journey, the inevitable consequence of reawakening into vibrational awareness is organic. It is like watering a plant. When we water a plant, we do not have to figure out how to make it grow. We do not even have to understand anything of the mechanisms of its ability to grow. When a plant receives the required attention, its growth is an automatic consequence. Similarly, when watered with the required conscious attention, the mind automatically ripens and blossoms as an expression of vibrational awareness.

The Breath of Life

WE human beings are distinguishable in that we are the only breathing creatures upon the face of the earth who *unconsciously* control our breathing. This unconscious control over our breathing mechanism manifests as long gaps between our in-breath and our out-breath. We may call this condition "pausing."

Habitual pausing is a consequence of not consciously residing in the body, but of residing primarily in the mental plane where our attention wanders out of this moment and into what we call the "past" and the "future." We seldom breathe while journeying through the mental plane, as there is no breath in the past and there is no breath in the future. Pausing between breaths is also a consequence of talking so much.

Observe a dog or cat. If the dog or cat has not begun to reflect its owner's dysfunctional behavior, it breathes without pausing. Observe a human being while they are on the telephone or watching television. There is little or no connected breathing. When a dog becomes frightened it breathes faster. When we humans become frightened, we hold our breath—literally stopping breathing altogether.

Our predicament is that we have a disconnected breathing mechanism. This manifestation is directly related to spending much of our waking experience in the mental plane—in a reflected past and a projected future.

Breathing dysfunctionally appears so normal to us that we are not even aware we are doing it. Living in a state of constant oxygen deprivation is now our normal state.

Being

THERE is something the mental body cannot grasp, no matter how much it tries to understand it.

No *doing* can activate the experience we call "being." No doing can increase the possibility of, enable, or add to the experience of being.

The resonance we call being continually permeates all doing, whether it is seen or unseen, realized or unrealized. The resonance we call being emanated before any doing was ever set in motion, and continues to emanate after every act of doing inevitably re-enters stillness, silence, and invisibility.

There is no doing that can add anything to, or take away anything from, the resonance of being. Our doings can simply cover up, or invite in, an awareness of the *beingness* that always is.

Not-Doing

DOINGS that are specifically intended to invite in the awareness of *being* are called "not-doings," or "un-doings."

To illustrate the purpose of a "not-doing," bring to mind the image of a sealed glass jar filled halfway with water, then topped up with oil. For the purpose of this illustration, the water represents our authentic vibrational essence—the unchanging *being* having the experience. The oil represents our physical, mental, and emotional attributes—the constantly changing experience we are having.

Much of our activity on earth is driven by a "need" to bring ease to the discomfort caused by the buildup of heat within our emotional body. We do not even know we are engaging in this behavior because we do not have the in-sight of emotional body awareness that would enable us to perceive the impact an imbalanced emotional body has on the overall quality of our life experience.

Without emotional body awareness, we behave backwards. We fiddle with effects in an effort to make causal impacts on the quality of our experience. We attempt to adjust our experience by rearranging our circumstances and by engaging in a lot of thinking, calculation, and analysis. This perceptual error is the cause of most of our doings.

But all that these doings accomplish is to constantly shake the jar of oil and water. As long as we believe we can add doings to our life experience as a means to transform the quality of our experience, all we accomplish is more shaking up of the jar. Consequently, the oil and water are so shaken up, they become one dull liquid, and so we can no longer tell the difference between what we are (the water) and the experience we are having (the oil).

A *not-doing* is any activity that empowers us to put the jar down and leave it alone. By allowing the jar to enter stillness, the oil and water automatically separate. A *not-doing* may be any ordinary aspect of our experience, like breathing, that we imbue with awareness as a means to consciously awaken to our authentic state of being.

Consciously Connected Breathing

THERE are many activities that may be wielded as not-doings. In fact, any life activity entered with the presence of observant attention becomes a not-doing, and therefore a vehicle to real eyes being.

Consciously connecting our breathing is a powerful not-doing because it enables our awareness to commence exiting the time-based illusions of the mental plane and reenter the presence of the physical body. As a *not-doing*, it empowers us to *undo*.

Consciously connected breathing is an elaborate way of describing the mechanics of breathing without pausing between the in-breath and the out-breath. It is not a fancy or complex practice. It is not even a practice! It is simply the act of breathing in and out of our nose, or in and out of our mouth, in a natural manner. It is so natural and ordinary that, when we engage in it, no one notices we are doing it. If, while we are consciously connecting our breathing, someone does notice that we are doing "something," then whatever it is we are doing is not what is being discussed here.

Try it now. Breathe normally in and out, without any large gaps or pauses between the in-breath and the out-breath. It is so simple.

Unless we are specifically looking for it, we do not notice a cat breathing, do we? This is the approach we are to have to consciously connected breathing—natural, unpretentious, and effortless.

Yes, we can transform this not-doing into a practice by deliberately breathing *much* fuller and deeper, in a manner that attracts attention from anyone in close proximity to us. We can breathe so loudly that others may hear we are deliberately working with our breath. We can sit in a lotus position so that others are alerted that we are about to do something "spiritual." But by doing this, we automatically turn a not-doing into a doing. We do not want to do this! One of the attributes of a not-doing is that no one notices we are doing it.

We are already breathing, so we are not adding anything to our current experience. We are merely adding awareness to an activity we are already involved in.

Consciously connected breathing is our normal breathing pattern attended to consciously. To make it more physically complicated by getting involved in a specific posture, or affecting the frequency and intensity of our breathing, or by focusing on the exact placement of our breath in the body, is to turn this into a doing.

Note: Consciously connected breathing as it is being discussed in this text is not "a practice" as it is applied in *The Presence Process*. That application of our breathing is part of a procedure, whereas this application is a seamless moment of increased awareness that is inserted into any aspect of our waking experience for as long as we choose.

The Impact of Presence

WHEN we consciously connect our breathing, an aspect of our aware-ness has to remain present in order to oversee this deliberate intent to focus our awareness on our breath.

The moment our attention slips back into a time-based paradigm, into our unconscious mental processes, we automatically begin pausing again. By not allowing ourselves to pause, by consciously connecting our breathing at random moments during our waking hours, we delib-erately activate increased presence awareness.

Consciously connected breathing reconnects our awareness to the circuitry of the life current that only flows within the present moment. It is this simple and powerful. Consciously connected breathing is one of the most efficient and accessible means for deliberate re-entry into the physical body. For every second we consciously connect our breathing, we are deliberately anchoring our awareness in the body, and therefore in the present moment. As simple as this not-doing is, and as normal as it appears, it has profound consequences.

To the mental body, consciously connecting our breathing appears too simplistic and nowhere near enough of an investment of intricate thought and energy to accomplish anything real and meaningful. The mental body assumes this not-doing is futile because it spends every waking and sleeping moment running all over the place within its com-plex understandings. In an attempt to accomplish the integration of mind, it initiates all sorts of intricate and effort-driven physical doings based on these understandings. Yet, through all eternity, it accomplishes absolutely nothing. It only "thinks" it does.

The mental body may ask: How can breathing normally accomplish anything? The mental body only asks a question like this because it has no capacity to comprehend the causal impact of an increase of presence upon the overall quality of our life experience.

The Best Kept Secret

THERE is a statistical relationship between various aspects of our human experience that is well worth visiting for a moment.

It is said we only use about 13% of our lung capacity. This means we are severely oxygen deprived! It is said we only use about 13% of our brain capacity. This means that for the most part we are really stupid! It is said we are only about 13% aware of what is happening within our human experience in any given moment, and that most of our awareness functions unconsciously. This means that we are for the most part fast asleep! It is said that barely 13% of our DNA is active. The rest of the inactive DNA is called "junk" DNA and appears to have no application. This means we are definitely not "firing on all cylinders!"

This is an interesting statistical correlation. (Yes, an artistic liberty has been taken in using the numerical value of 13 in all the percentages. It is definitely way too high in each of the above instances.)

It would be *in effect you all* for us to get up one morning and declare, "That's it! I am done firing on practically no cylinders. Today I am going to activate all my DNA strands!" Good luck with this.

It would also be equally *in effect you all* for us to get up one morning and declare, "That's it! I am done behaving unconsciously. Today I am going to be 100% aware!" Good luck with this, too.

It would be just as *in effect you all* for us to get up one morning and declare, "That's it! I am done being stupid. Today I am functioning with full brain capacity!" Good luck with this, also.

However, it is not at all far-fetched to declare, "Today I am going to spend a little more time during my day consciously connecting my breathing."

When we start consistently and consciously connecting our breathing randomly throughout our day, we experience unexpected consequences:

- We start understanding that which made no sense to us before, as if we are beginning to use more of our brain.

- We start noticing aspects of our experience previously invisible to our perception, as if we are suddenly gaining awareness.

- We start having whole and complete integrated in-sights that explode into our mind's eye as instantaneously as a light bulb being turned on, like the firing up of a once-disconnected cylinder—or DNA strand.

All these shifts start unfolding simply because we are breathing consciously and consistently. Not breathing madly, not breathing compulsively, and not breathing desperately, but gently, naturally, and most importantly, *consistently*.

Oxygen: Take consciously and consistently every day. It is nature's best-kept secret, yet it is so readily available that even the pharmaceutical companies cannot patent and control it. Side effects include increased intelligence, awareness, insight, and integration.

Awakening the Unconscious

WHEN we consciously connect our breathing, an aspect of our awareness that is unconsciously addicted to entering the mental plane with the intent to try and understand "what happened" and "how to stop whatever it was that happened from happening again" becomes anchored in the present moment.

The consequence of this anchoring of attention, of this increase of presence awareness, is that the unintegrated energetic condition around which this aspect of our awareness has been unconsciously buzzing no longer receives its regular dose of attention.

Like a needy and wanting child that does not get what it wants, or a festering habit that is not fed, this energetic condition starts to react. Because our awareness is no longer unconsciously tending to it as an accomplice of the mind's desire for integration, this unintegrated energy begins to vibrate in a manner that causes it to surface into our conscious awareness. Like any habit if we do not feed it, it comes looking for food.

As this unconscious causal condition surfaces into our awareness, it follows the energetic flow as dictated by The Pathway of Awareness whenever we consciously approach the vibrational. Remember, we are now deliberately engaging a journey in which we are consciously retracing the energetic steps we took along The Pathway of Awareness. Consequently, the energetic flow of our journey from this point onward in the text is from physical to mental to emotional, with the intent to enter an experiential conversation with the vibrational.

When we deliberately anchor an aspect of our awareness in the present moment through a not-doing like consciously connected breathing, the unconscious energetic circumstance that once addictively absorbed this aspect of our awareness first rises into our field of experience as unfamiliar and uncomfortable *physical* sensations, then as convincing *mental* stories, and finally as fearful, angry, and grieving *emotional* signatures.

⟨ 11 ⟩

From Enemy to Ally

A<small>T</small> this point in our adventure, it is crucial that we adjust our perceptual relationship with what we call "pain and discomfort."

We have been trained through the example of others to assume that pain and discomfort come to hurt us and must therefore be stamped out at all cost. Accordingly, we instinctively react to the emergence of pain and discomfort by controlling it, sedating it, cutting it out, or drugging it. We "do" whatever it takes to eliminate our awareness of it. This perceptual error often has dire and sometimes fatal consequences.

Pain and discomfort do not come to hurt us; they come to reveal where we are already hurting. Pain and discomfort do not cause suffering. Reacting to our pain and discomfort as if something is wrong causes suffering.

Suffering is the consequence of sedating and controlling our pain and discomfort. It comes from attempting to numb the communications coming from our emotional body, which are reflected as uncomfortable sensations within our physical and mental body.

In this respect, the pain triggered through a not-doing is not an enemy. It is an ally.

Pain Is a Portal

ONE of the first things awoken through a not-doing practice like consciously connected breathing is an awareness of uncomfortable sensations within our physical body. These sensations mirror the energetic imbalances within our emotional body.

These uncomfortable physical sensations are messengers and allies whose *soul task* is to guide us toward reestablishing a conversation with the unspeakable. *Our* task is to feel them without trying to change them into anything else.

They may arise as aches, cramps, hot flashes, dull pains, and as all manner of unfamiliar physical sensations. By *feeling* our pain and discomfort without censoring it, we awaken our ability to feel. Being willing to feel our physical pain and discomfort is the first step toward rekindling emotional body awareness.

In this light, the unfamiliar physical sensations arising through not-doings like consciously connected breathing are portals. They are a rite of passage into reawakening emotional body awareness. They are the right passageway through which to reenter felt-perception of the heart.

Once we become comfortable with our own physical discomfort, we automatically move along The Pathway of Awareness from physical to mental. We open ourselves to receiving in-sight from our heart about the authentic condition of our emotional body.

Perceptual Tools

ONCE our intent to regain physical presence is set, the next step is to move inward along The Pathway of Awareness by inviting mental clarity. Activating mental clarity requires the same "not-doing" approach as we initiate through consciously connected breathing.

One of the most powerful means of accomplishing mental clarity is with perceptual tools. A perceptual tool is a thought form that invites us to approach our life experience differently, that's all. It is to perceive our life experience from a deliberately altered point of view, and then to observe the consequences. The entire text of this book is a mega perceptual tool made up of many perceptual tools. Simply by reading this text, our perception—and hence our point of view—is irreversibly altered.

For example, The Pathway of Awareness is a perceptual tool. Once we see the movement of this energetic pathway within the dynamics of our own life experience, we cannot un-see it. The Seven Year Cycle is also a perceptual tool. Once we see its cyclic unfolding within the dynamics of our own life experience, we cannot un-see it.

A perceptual tool transforms the mental body into an altar.

To accomplish perceptual transformation we need "do" nothing. It is activated purely by the conscious wielding of our attention and intention.

A perceptual tool *opens* something—it facilitates *an opening* within our awareness that is "unspeakable." This opening is a feeling, and this feeling is a portal into an awareness of our majestic identity.

Closing the Opening

JUST as the mental body may be an ally in facilitating an opening, if it is allowed to run the show it can also downgrade the experience of the opening into the numbness of unconsciousness.

Let us observe an example of how the mental body does this by examining the word "beautiful." According to the mental body, the meaning of this word has something to do with appearances that are pleasurable to the mind. However, if we explore the word phonetically and slowly speak the phrase *be you 'til full*—"be you 'til full"—and then again mouth the word "beautiful," suddenly the word causes the feeling of *an opening* within us. The impact of this opening is in the feeling it initiates.

If we are as mental as most of us humans have become, we push aside the initial felt-experience of the opening and immediately ask ourselves how many other words in the English language we can do this exercise with. We then become lost within mental body analysis and are no longer in the moment into which the opening invited us.

This illustrates how a perceptual tool can be an ally or a distraction. It all depends on the quality of our intent. Do we allow ourselves to rest within the opening, or do we quickly shut ourselves down by engaging in endless mental examination and complexity?

Let us experience this again. Take the word "surrender," and then examine the phrase *sure ender*. Or take the word "intimacy," and then examine the phrase *into me and see*. Do we allow ourselves to feel the opening these words invite once we are aware of the phrases imbedded within them? Or is our mental body already wondering what other words in the English language are constructed in this manner?

Wake up! Every aspect of creation is imbedded with progressively deeper levels of illuminating intelligence! All of life is an opening. However, these portals are hidden from those of us who have become completely mental about everything.

These doorways, though recognized through a conscious wielding of the mental body, only allow passage into deeper awareness when entry is made with felt-perception. The core of any adjustment made through a perceptual tool arises not out of mental understanding, but out of felt-impact.

Mental Clarity

MENTAL clarity rests upon two prime realizations. The first is that the quality of our life experience is determined by the condition of our emotional body. The second is that we are personally responsible for the condition of our emotional body.

As we have already pointed out, others can do physical tasks on our behalf. They can mail letters for us, move objects around for us, and even pick us up and carry us if they are strong enough. Mentally, others can also perform tasks on our behalf. They can do research and communicate it for us, and even think out strategies on our behalf. But when it comes to our emotions, no one can feel on our behalf. Anyone who claims they can is deluded.

As we have also shown, the quality of our experience is determined by the way we *feel* about our experience, which in itself is determined by the condition of our emotional body in any given moment.

It does not matter what the physical circumstances are, or what we tell ourselves conceptually about our experience, the reality is that no matter how much we move objects around upon earth, and no matter how much we think about and analyze any situation, if we do not *feel* comfortable within it, we are not comfortable within it. If we seek to regain an awareness of peace, this is only accomplished when we *feel* peace. And we—and no one else—hold the reins on our capacity to do so.

The moment this realization sinks in is the moment we stop using our mental body as a means to think and *anal eyes* our way out of discomfort and back into an awareness of peace. Then we begin wielding our mental body at its highest frequency—as a tool for navigation.

Information Is Not Knowledge

INFORMATION is not knowledge. But because of our exaggerated mental state, we currently live in a perceptual condition in which we mistakenly confuse information with knowledge.

Information only transforms into knowledge when it is combined with *experience*. When we act from this point of awareness—from information + experience = knowledge—only then do we activate the resonance called *wisdom*.

Telling ourselves mentally that *the quality of our life experience is determined by the condition of our emotional body,* and that *we are responsible for the condition of our emotional body,* is not enough. Even when we arrive at this point of understanding through intelligent deductive reasoning, as we have done so far, it is still not enough. For the mental body to become satisfied that this is indeed true, so that it will release its grasp of domination and control, we must place this information upon the altar of experience.

What makes an experience "an experience" is that it contains the complete trinity of the integrated mind within it—the physical, mental, and emotional components. The resonance called "knowing" that transforms words from mental chatter—from information into actual knowledge—occurs when the physical and emotional components are added to the mental.

This is why four years of book study and verbal lectures at a college or university are only guaranteed to turn out mental people—individuals overloaded with information, but deprived of the experiential container of physical and emotional interaction required to transform accumulated data into authentic *knowledge*.

Take the Ride

IF we are asked to give a verbal presentation on a roller coaster, there are a number of ways we may approach this:

—*1*—

We may spend a day in a theme park watching a roller coaster. After this we may talk about a roller coaster from the point of observation—from being in the physical presence of one.

—*2*—

We may go to a library and take out a book on g-force and the engineering parameters which go into manufacturing roller coasters. After this mental investigation, we may talk about the subject according to accumulated information—according to our mental grasp of it.

—*3*—

We may take a five-minute ride on a roller coaster.

Guess which talk may be somewhat boring? Guess which talk captures another's attention? Guess which talk inspires another to take a ride on a roller coaster? Guess which talk comes from the resonance of personal knowledge? Guess which talk comes from the heart and which comes from the head?

Of course, we could do all three—observe, study, and enter the experience. Such a holistic approach to any subject makes for a truly integrated discussion. However, leave out the actual ride, the actual experience, and we become lost in the mental realm's endless passageways of information.

Wisdom is born when we real eyes that:

information + experience = knowledge.

"How" Is Control

WHEN we say that the quality of our life experience is determined by the condition of our emotional body, and that we are responsible for the condition of our emotional body, it is important that we give ourselves the opportunity to back up this assertion with a real experience. This experience may be easily accumulated by consciously navigating any aspect of our daily life.

Let us cite an example of navigating our experience by imagining we are taking a flight from New York to South Africa. Such a flight is a long trip, and long trips can leave one feeling really exhausted upon arrival. The possibility of arriving exhausted may encourage us to control our experience in an attempt to arrive in a more favorable condition. However, if we attempt to control the many aspects of this experience in order to force a desired outcome, we are likely to be even more exhausted at the outcome! Controlling everything is in itself an exhausting occupation.

What is it that we are trying to accomplish when we resort to control? The aspects of any experience that we seek to control all lie in the *how* of the experience.

Take note that whenever anyone tells us about challenges they are facing in their life, they regularly use the word *how*. The difficulty of life always lies in *the how*. "How am I going to do this?" or "How am I going to do that?"

This "how" dilemma only arises because we are always attempting to do everything ourselves. We have little or no faith in the causal point of the quality of our experience. In fact, for the most part, we do not even know that there is a causal point to the quality of our experience, because as long as we are physically trance fixed and mentally entangled, we believe our experience is happening *to* us, not *through* us. Consequently, we habitually resort to control as a means of defending ourselves from points of discomfort that appear to be imposing themselves upon our experience.

Whenever we use the word "how" in relation to a problem we are having, what we are actually saying is: How do I control what is happening to me and around me?

‹ I 2 ›

Navigating Our Experiences

THERE is an approach to facing life's challenges consciously that is as old as the trees, yet we only become aware of it when we real eyes the significance of the felt-component in determining the quality of our human experience.

To illustrate the mechanics of this approach, we return to our example of catching a flight from New York to South Africa. Once we know we are definitely booked on the flight, we may determine to take responsibility for the experience by consciously navigating it. Navigation, as we have already mentioned, is the noblest use of our mental body.

We apply the art of conscious navigation by honoring the flow of the energetic movement within The Pathway of Awareness that we always use when manifesting our experiences upon this earth—from emotional to mental to physical.

STEP ONE:
WE PLACE OUR ATTENTION AT THE OUTCOME OF OUR EXPERIENCE, AT THE POINT AT WHICH WE ARE DISEMBARKING FROM THE PLANE AND STEPPING INTO OLIVER TAMBO INTERNATIONAL AIRPORT IN SOUTH AFRICA. AS WE SEE OURSELVES ARRIVING THERE, OVER THIS VISUALIZATION WE PLACE A FEELING—*THE WAY WE CHOOSE TO FEEL AT THE OUTCOME OF OUR JOURNEY.* We may choose to feel relaxed, renewed, and in good spirits. The most important aspect of this first step in our navigational procedure is that as we visualize ourselves arriving in South Africa, we must simultaneously bring that intended feeling we seek at the outcome of our journey into our awareness *now.* If we cannot feel that intended

feeling *now,* how do we expect to feel it when we actually arrive in "the now" of that visualized moment? (There is only now.) Once we can visualize ourselves arriving at our destination and simultaneously place this feeling over this picture by feeling this way now, we immediately let it go. We must not dwell upon this first step. We must not concentrate deeply upon this intent. We effortlessly see it, feel it, and let it go. Effortlessness comes from effortlessness. The only time we return to this step is if and when we experience anxiety about the upcoming flight. When we catch ourselves entertaining this unconscious behavior—anxiety—we place our attention within the field of anxiety and feel this rising discomfort without any attempt to change or transform it. We allow it to be. After a few moments, we gently overlay it with our navigated felt-request. Then we again effortlessly let it go.

STEP TWO:

We make sure we have all the mental information we require for our journey. This may include the time of departure, flight number, confirmation number, and information about visas if this is required.

STEP THREE:

We make sure we are physically prepared to embark upon this journey. We pack, make sure we have our passport and ticket, etc.

STEP FOUR:

When our day of travel arrives, we step into the experience and allow it to unfold without agenda, control, or interference. We go with the flow of it, whether we perceive it flowing in our favor or not. We surrender—we end being sure. This is a challenging part because, in order for the experience to deliver us to our navigated outcome, we have to discard all our assumptions about how it is going to unfold. We must get out of our own way! *From the moment we enter the navigated experience, any and all unexpected discomfort is the universe rearranging circumstances so that we may experience the intended out-*

come. If we interfere—*enter fear*—with the unfolding of the experience, we sabotage our intended outcome. When we get out of our own
way, we witness a seemingly invisible force arranging circumstances
in a manner we could not possibly have orchestrated or facilitated.
Once we have seen the universe at play in this manner, we real eyes
that if we navigate our experiences consciously, and then allow them
to unfold without interference, the "how" is orchestrated by the universe. This is the miracle. What God is to us is the "how." Allowing the
how of the experience to be placed within the hands of the universe
invites *what God is for us* to partner with us, as a co-creator of our experiences.

The Child Is a Creator

THE child is created in the "image of God," and the child is the emotional body. When we consciously work with and allow the child—the emotional body—to operate as the causal point of our experiences, we allow a force that is omnipresent, omniscient, and omni-powerful to join in as a co-creative member of our manifestation team.

The reverse also applies. When we unconsciously allow the child—the emotional body—to operate as the causal point of our experiences, we allow a force that is omnipresent, omniscient, and omni-powerful to manifest the quality of our experiences based on the unintegrated and imprinted condition of a seven-year-old.

A word of warning. We are only to navigate the outcome of our experiences through felt-content, and not through a request for specific mental details and physical parameters. What God is to us is initially only tangible to us in the feeling. It is therefore through the parameter of feeling that we most efficiently converse with our creative source.

Details serve only to bedevil us by allowing the mental body to impose its heartless willfulness.

Experience As Our Teacher

THE four-step navigational procedure WE have just illustrated may be used for navigating any and all experiences. We may use it to navigate the felt-outcome of each day, of business meetings, of conflict resolution, of any experience we are aware we are entering.

When we real eyes we can manifest any feeling we request as an outcome by consciously navigating our experiences, and that by arriving at that intended outcome we are predetermining the quality of the experience, then through personal experience we know physically, mentally, and emotionally that the quality of our life experience is determined by the condition of our emotional body, and that we are responsible for the condition of our emotional body. In this manner, our life experience becomes our teacher. We have metaphorically climbed aboard the roller coaster, taken the ride, and allowed the experience to be our guide.

The moment we bless our human encounters with the responsibility inherent in consciously navigating our life experiences, by working causally with the emotional body and seeing the miracle of this, we are ready to begin curbing our endless thinking and anal-eyes-ing. Then we are ready to accept that the mental body is a bridge to be crossed, a corridor to be moved through, and a passageway leading us to the heart of the matter.

At this point in our journey, we set our intent to discover the authentic condition of the emotional body, to restore its balance, and to explore its role in facilitating an experiential conversation with the unspeakable.

The Lost Key

NOTICE that beneath all our confused and repetitive thinking, there is an energetic "noise"—an uncomfortable resonance that can be clearly felt when our attention is placed on it. Within this text, we call this a dysfunctional emotional signature.

When we embrace *experience as a teacher,* we fast real eyes it is no use attempting to forcefully change or stop our confused and repetitive thinking without first paying attention to the dysfunctional emotional signature that underlies it. This is because, according to The Pathway of Awareness, our thinking is driven by the condition of our emotional body.

Instead of trying to mentally force a change in our thinking, it is more efficient to focus our time and energy on awakening to, and then consciously adjusting, the dysfunctional emotional signature beneath these thoughts. When we access and adjust the dysfunctional emotional signature, the thought processes we are struggling with automatically transform to reflect this causal adjustment.

Approaching our experience in this manner is imbued with integrity. We are efficiently impacting the quality of our human experience because we are aware of the correct application of the components that manifest it.

Once we initiate this level of personal responsibility, we are ready to awaken to the authentic resonance of *intimacy.*

Healing

FROM this point onward within this text, when we use the word "healing," we are specifically referring to the conscious felt-adjustment of the imprinted dysfunction within the emotional body.

When radiated unconsciously from the emotional body into the mental and physical parameters of our experience, this imprinted dysfunction manifests as symptomatic experiences such as accidents, diseases, and addictions.

When we use the word "healing," we are not referring to physically attending to wounds or symptoms, or to mentally discussing a diagnosis. We are referring to the precise moment in which we energetically impact *the causal point* of any outer physical and mental state of discomfort through felt-perception.

Feeling Is Healing

BECAUSE the energetic condition of the emotional body is defined within us through imprinting by the age of seven, we may metaphorically view this attribute of our experience as the "child." Being childlike, it is simple, not complex. It feels, and it accomplishes everything through feeling.

The moment we restore balance within our emotional body, this adjusted energetic condition is automatically radiated outward along The Pathway of Awareness into our mental processes and physical circumstances. Restoring balance within our emotional body requires only one intent—*to feel what is*. The mental body, scratching its head in disbelief, wants to ask, "How can this possibly be?"

Let us illustrate how the emotional body restores balance through "feeling what is." We will use standing up, balanced on our own two feet, as a metaphor for a healthy, emotionally balanced human experience.

If we stand with our hands by our sides, eyes closed, and allow ourselves to gradually start falling forward, beyond a certain point we completely lose balance, fall over, and hit the ground. This experience of hitting the ground is akin to the development of a *symptom* of imbalance. It represents a piece of unintegrated time that may manifest within our life experience as an accident, disease, or addiction.

The reason we fall forwards or backwards to the point that we hit the ground is because we are unable to feel how out of balance we are. In other words, we lose balance because we have a diminished capacity to feel—a lack of emotional body awareness.

As we are falling, we may attempt to counteract this circumstance mentally by opening our eyes, observing the changing angle of our falling body, and saying, "I am five degrees off balance and gradually moving further off balance by 2.58 degrees per 3.29 milliseconds. To regain my balance, I best move my weight in the opposite direction by 1.99 degrees every 1.45 milliseconds." This approach of mentally calculating our predicament, and then making physical adjustments according to these mental calculations, illustrates the task we have placed in the lap of traditional therapy and psychiatry.

When we only invest our energy in this mental approach of thinking and analysis, no matter how precisely we calculate our predicament or chart our method of recovery, we still continue to fall. This is because *when we are thinking about our condition, we are not feeling*.

It is extremely difficult to think and feel at the same time. Even with our eyes wide open, thinking and analysis—because they numb our ability to feel—inevitably lead us into losing balance, falling further, and ending up on the ground. When we approach an imbalanced aspect of our human experience only through our mental body, the consequences are *in effect you all*.

The same is true of approaching an imbalanced human experience only physically. Once we are off balance, no amount of flailing our arms or adjusting our posture can help us. In fact, beyond a certain point of imbalance, the more we physically engage our symptomatic experience with treatment and pharmaceuticals, the more likely we are to hasten the moment of hitting the ground.

By reawakening our ability to feel what is happening in the moment, and by trusting the impetus of our feelings, even with our eyes shut, we are able to feel how far over we are leaning and automatically counter this momentum in such a way as to restore our balance. We do not require any thinking to accomplish this, nor do we require visibly seeing our physical circumstances. Simply *feeling how out of balance we are* empowers us to restore our balance.

This illustration may be simplistic, but it reveals a simple secret concerning the functioning of the emotional body. When we allow ourselves to feel the authentic condition of our emotional body, without trying to change what we are feeling, we empower the emotional body to enter the process of restoring balance. We enable the suppressed energetic circumstances we have conceptually labeled as fear, anger, and grief to reenter motion so they may reach completion and bring about integration.

It is this simple. To make it any more complex than this is to become mental. Feeling is healing.

Healing As Causal

WHEN we only rely on the capacities of the mental or physical aspect of our experience to heal our suffering, we inevitably make the experience of healing, or becoming whole again, unnecessarily complex.

This is because, alone, neither the physical nor mental component of our human experience has the capacity to facilitate the moment of healing.

The physical may reflect to us what requires healing. The mental may empower us to decipher the reflections perceived within the physical, and then to navigate our attention to the causal point of the symptom. But both are left speechless once the diagnosis is delivered and the causal point uncovered. From this point onward, only felt-perception of the heart is useful.

When we do not real eyes this, and therefore make healing the task of the physical body, we invariably become exhausted from all the intricate procedures and postures we entertain. Before we real eyes what we are doing, we are giving ourselves coffee enemas, or standing on one leg sipping a blend of carrot and mustard juice while trying to breathe a smile through our left kidney. Alternatively, we retreat into the sedation and control of pharmaceuticals.

The physical aspect of our human experience can only help us to *re-cover*—to sedate and control our symptoms through covering them up. The physical aspect of our human experience cannot, through recovery, heal anything in and of itself. It can efficiently attend to wounds and address the symptoms of disease and discomfort, but it cannot address the causal point.

Likewise, if we make healing the task of the mental body, it too becomes frustrated and begins making up stories, designing complex procedures, labeling symptoms with fancy Latin names, and imagining all manner of illusionary causes for and outcomes to our predicament.

Before we real eyes what we are doing, we are condemning ourselves to lifelong symptoms, trying to "activate our Merkabah" or "reconfigure our light body," or engaging in some ungrounded and fantastical mental entanglement. This is because the mental aspect of our human experience cannot heal anything in and of itself. It is able to participate in facilitating successful diagnosis, and in directing the focus of our attention to the causal point of the condition, but it is not a healer.

Neither the mental nor physical body is a healer. They express what requires healing, facilitate the recovery of symptoms, deliver attention to the point at which healing is required, and then radiate the consequences of healing when it is accomplished through felt-perception. They are not causal, they are attendants.

Because our emotional body is the causal point of the quality of our experience, healing—or returning to an awareness of our inherent wholeness—is initiated by the heart directly through our emotional body via felt-perception.

‹ 13 ›

Fear, Anger, and Grief

As we consciously enter and journey through the authentic condition of our emotional body, we travel along the Pathway of Awareness the same way as when we pray or seek to know what God is for us. We move from physical to mental to emotional. Because of this, our movement through the dysfunctional resonances of the emotional body is from fear (physical) to anger (mental) to grief (emotional).

FEAR IS ROOTED WITHIN OUR PHYSICAL EXPERIENCE.
Fear relates to our attachment to the body, to matter, and to our confined sense of mortality that comes from this attachment. We are most afraid of being physically injured, hurt, and dying. Behind all our fear is the word "death." This idea, that *we* can die, is founded on being physically trance fixed by the physical aspects of our experience. We identify with our physical experience instead of with our vibrational experience. Energetically, fear is a name we give to any circumstances we do not recognize and for which we have no point of reference. Until we integrate our fear, we have no capacity for discernment.

ANGER IS ROOTED WITHIN OUR MENTAL EXPERIENCE.
Anger relates to revenge, and revenge is always hooked to a mental plot. Anger is rooted in the story we tell ourselves, in which the plotline attributes our circumstances to outer factors. Anger is the mental fuel igniting all blame and judgment. It fractures our thought forms and shatters all mental clarity. Underlying all anger is the assumption we are either victims or victors. It is rooted in an assumption our life

experience is happening *to us,* and we are therefore essentially not responsible for it. Energetically, anger is a name we give to any circumstance we do not know how to manage. Until we integrate our anger, we cannot assert ourselves in a healthy manner. We can only attempt to assert ourselves in a manner that is aggressive. We have no capacity to assert ourselves in a calm and centered way that reflects true awareness and presence.

GRIEF IS ROOTED WITHIN OUR EMOTIONAL EXPERIENCE.
Grief relates to a deep sorrow and is always hooked directly into a feeling of somehow having "missed the boat" or "missed the mark." It points to something deep within us that appears lost or missing. Energetically, grief is a name we give to any circumstance we are holding onto that we do not know how to let go of, or any experience we expected to manifest that did not materialize. Until we integrate our grief, we do not have the capacity to feel deeply without losing balance.

Fear Is the Key

FEAR is the energetic condition that separates the wheat from the chaff. This is because we cannot face our fears simply to please someone else. We cannot enter our own fear authentically other than through intent to do so for ourselves.

Until we authentically address our fear, we do not authentically unveil our anger and grief, which are even more challenging to integrate.

Therefore, if we are not yet ready to face our fear, it means we are not yet ready to face our anger and grief.

Shying away from our fear automatically shields us from entering the part of our evolutionary journey that empowers us to enter a conversation with the unspeakable. In this light, our fear is a deliberate gatekeeper. This is why it is said, "Fear is the key."

Why Are We Afraid?

IT is not really our personally suppressed fear that determines whether or not we are ready to embark upon the work that empowers us to grow up emotionally. It is the fear we have of our own unintegrated fear.

Yet, our unintegrated fear is nothing; it is *no thing*.

Our unconscious fears are made up of ghostly memories and phantom projections. Our personally suppressed and unintegrated fears, as we mentally interact with them, are thought forms about that which has already happened, or about that which has not yet happened. They have no reality to them in this moment.

Once we allow ourselves to sink into our suppressed fear, without attempting to change it—without attempting to turn it from "tangled and knotted balls of bleeding black barbed wire into celestial bubbles of radiant angelic swansong," or any of that silly nonsense—we inevitably discover what we most fear.

Our greatest fear is of our own anger and the rageful consequences of allowing ourselves to express it fully. We are afraid that if we allow ourselves to openly express the extent of our rage, we may destroy this whole earth!

Why Are We Angry?

WHEN we allow ourselves to sit in the midst of our anger, without sedating or controlling the intensity of the experience—without telling stories and projecting it outward toward others—we soon discover why we are so angry. We are angry because we had our heart broken.

As children, we radiated innocently and unconditionally into our life experience, and often the beauty of our radiance was not reflected within our experiences. We all entered this life as unconditional vibrational beings, and the process of entering a conditional emotional, mental, and physical experience is heartbreaking for an unconditional being.

We are now angry about our unseen shift from presence to pretence.

We are angry about having to become "well-behaved," standing statue-still with barely one toe moving when the circumstances of life call for jubilant dancing and chanting.

We are furious at addictively being incarcerated by consistently doing the "right" thing and the "expected" thing to make it in the calculated and pretentious adult world.

We are exhausted from "playing it safe" and having to come across as "a nice person" so we do not "upset anyone" or "cause unnecessary conflict."

Within us there is a child bound by order, control, sedation, expectation, judgment, and self-denial. Our anger is this child screaming for air and sunlight from within the dungeon of our forgotten heart.

Whenever we self-medicate, we are practicing internalized child abuse.

Friction Is Movement

ANGER is the most challenging of the three emotionaldiscomforts to integrate. This is because in the adult world we are permitted and even encouraged to feel afraid. We are allowed to purchase guns, to rig our homes with security systems, and to worship crime, war, and "terror" as the motivation behind our life choices.

In the adult world it is not permitted to be sad. We have developed an entire range of pharmaceuticals to pander to our grief.

Because we have no outlet for our rage, most of us turn this rage inward and develop various degrees of emotional paralysis that huddle together under the umbrella of "depression." We have a range of pharmaceuticals for this too.

Violent crime is a projection of this inwardly injected venom spewing outward upon the planet. So too is our fascination with and continued participation in war.

Any vehicle requiring forward momentum relies on the friction beneath its wheels to grip and propel it forward. It also relies on the friction of the applied braking mechanism to bring it to a standstill. When we consciously or unconsciously entertain unintegrated anger, we live with our energetic brakes applied 24/7.

Consequently, there are large areas of our life in which we experience zero movement—paralysis. Any point within our life experience at which we feel "stuck" is a clue to a manifestation of our unintegrated anger. This state of energetic paralysis due to imploding rage is what depression is.

Yet, what we may not real eyes is that anger is also the most powerful and untapped attribute for movement within the emotional body.

Only when we consciously integrate our anger are we able to assert ourselves effectively within our life experience. Then, the very same friction that comes from living with the brakes on becomes the means for forward momentum—for transformation.

Unless we take care of the angry child within us, our life experi-ence remains dead in the water—and as long as we "play dead," we are unable to integrate the sadness underlying this anger.

Crying Without Reason

By sinking into the depths of our anger, we awaken to the resonance of an innocent child with a broken heart.

When we allow ourselves to fully express this suppressed grief, alone—without reasons, without having to know any of the childhood details of why we are feeling such sorrow, and without needing or even wanting someone else to comfort us and tell us "it will be all right"—we discover the majestic beauty of tears as detoxifying agents of the emotional body.

As we move through the many layers from fear to anger to grief, over and over again, we real eyes that these energetic circumstances, when sedated and controlled, become distorted lenses through which we perceive our experience of life on this earth.

As we embrace each of our unintegrated emotional states and allow ourselves to "be within them," we experience a perceptual transformation that completely adjusts the way we perceive life on earth. We move beyond the veil of yesterday's ghosts and tomorrow's phantoms, and real eyes *where* we really are.

It is only by moving consciously *through,* and gradually integrating, these unintegrated emotional conditions that we experientially comprehend why and how our emotional body is a "rite of passage" to achieving perceptual integration.

Dying to Live

THE consequence of embracing any not-doing that facilitates the undoing of our emotional imprinting is that we initiate and move through various resonances of physical, mental, and emotional cleansing that are perceived by us as uncomfortable.

This uncomfortable unsheathing of our current experience from the coverings of our unintegrated past is a conscious death experience—the death of what is not real so we may reenter the authentic resonance of the present moment.

Essentially, because the causal points of our present discomforts are anchored in the imprinted condition of our emotional body, this cleansing death experience is at its heart *an emotional death*.

Because we are physically trance fixed by the world, our current perception of death is that it is primarily a physical event. However, as we awaken into emotional body awareness, we real eyes death has more than one expression. When instructed by sacred texts to *die while living*, this does not pertain to a physical experience, but to our conscious entry into an ongoing receptivity to also experiencing mental and emotional deaths.

When we cleave the past, our stories we have *spelled* and *sentenced* ourselves to must die—and so too must the emotional signature in which they are rooted.

The Death Experience

THIS mental and emotional death experience comes to us organically in the days and weeks following any consistent application of a not-doing practice. Without any warning, it engulfs us as deeply uncomfortable states of being.

When these extremely uncomfortable states first impact us, we reel into unconsciousness. We reactively fight the experience, desperately trying our best to stop whatever is happening from happening. Through our reactivity, we attempt to escape emotionally, mentally, and physically from our encounter with "the reaper of the past and projected future."

As this death experience unfolds, we literally feel as if we are "dying," as if "there is nothing to live for"—that "our life is over," it is "hopeless to do anything," and we are condemned forever to these feelings of darkness, doom, and gloom.

Yet, within a relatively short period of time, within hours or sometimes days—depending on the immensity of the dysfunctional energetic experience we are dying to—this wave of momentary physical, mental, and emotional shedding of the skin of our past peels over us and is gone.

In its wake, we feel more awake, aware, inspired, and deeply grateful to be alive.

Dying Consciously Invites Rebirth

WHEN living an integrated life, these death experiences are perfectly normal, natural, healthy, and organic.

When we allow ourselves to go through this rite of passage, it becomes blatantly obvious that, in order to avoid these death experiences, we have taken off *en masse* into the mental plane. We have occupied ourselves with a mindless array of physical business.

It is precisely because our current culture is indoctrinated into believing death is an enemy that we run terrified and attempt to barricade ourselves mentally and physically from these experiences. From childhood, we are led to believe through imprinted example that the experience of death is a mistake, and so we run from it into our thoughts, spiritual practices, religious organizations, complex philosophies, and intricate psychological systems.

We have forgotten that to remain present within the turbulence of the human experience entails consistently dying emotionally and mentally to the illusionary constructs we have manufactured called *the past and the future.*

We have forgotten that rebirth and death cohabit the same reality—that they are two sides of the same coin. We have forgotten that all rebirth comes out of death—that a consciously-embraced death experience is the invited moment of rebirth. We have become a tree that clings to spring and summer, and denies the existence of fall and winter.

Religion Is a Barricade

ONE of the profound revelations we receive when consciously be-friending these death experiences is the realization that we have manufactured what we now call religion as a vain attempt to save us from having to face these uncomfortable states of rebirth. Our religious endeavors promise an eternity barricaded from the death experience.

This daily death we consciously initiate and invite when we face our unintegrated emotional content is closer to an authentic earth religion than many of the organized ways of worship we have today. More accurately, dying consciously while alive is an ancient shamanic experience—the exact experience shunned within communities whenever they are overtaken, overshadowed, and indoctrinated by any conservative and closed-hearted religious *mentality*.

Most of our religious organizations nowadays run toward God as a reaction to the unfathomable reality of life and not as a response to God. They are a way of implanting a false certainty into the unfathomable human experience, of avoiding a constant dying to the known, and an attempt to deny our never-ending plunge into the void.

For the most part, organized religion is a dance around the void— an *avoid-dance*.

This invited emotional and mental death—this conscious cleaving of the imprinted past—is not an avoidance.

Dying while living is a direct, in-the-moment response to whatever God is for us by facing and consciously dying to whatever we are placing between us and an authentic awareness of whatever God is for us. It is a conscious acknowledgement of the unfathomable darkness of the endlessly unfamiliar—the awesome, ever-changing, and unknowable face of God.

This invited and ongoing reoccurrence of *dying to the past* is a conscious sinking into the void, into the unfamiliar, into the uncomfortable and as yet unformed. This emotional and mental death is "a rising up through sinking in," like a Phoenix out of the ashes.

Jesus the Shaman

THE reality of this mental and emotional death experience was known and honored long before any church mentality outlawed all practices honoring it.

Because we have run in terror from this mental and emotional death experience, it now follows us into old age as a frightening shadow. In its wake, it leaves a trail of disease, unconscious accidental mishaps, addiction, and a quality of life that eventually culminates in an experience of demeaning decay and dismay.

Instead of dying daily, we now resist it with all our might and subsequently allow it to build up into a massive, culminating drama that explodes ungracefully when our moment of physical transition from Earth approaches.

Yet, when we consciously and willingly enter our heart, and face the shadow of our unintegrated past—when we consistently allow this past to physically, mentally, and emotionally die through us—we organically reawaken into an ancient shamanic rite of passage elevating us into a direct experience with whatever God is for us: the fullness of the present moment.

We discover that these waves of deathly discomfort that share the ocean of life with us are a holy blessing. They come to show us we must die consistently and consciously so that we may live fully. They come to strip us of the past so that each moment we step into is born anew.

These ongoing death experiences are the Christed moments through which all is born anew. These death experiences are the many crucifixions that take place before any legitimate ascension and reawakening into vibrational awareness. In revealing this secret to us so graphically, Jesus is a profound, planetary shaman.

The Juice of Life

THROUGH experientially embracing this death experience as integral to life, we discover it has been because of our avoidance of these death experiences that our heart has closed. Through our unconscious resistance to feeling this necessary rite of passage, we have desperately sought ascension—escape—through endless mental concepts and tedious physical behaviors and practices.

Yet, all that the mental and physical accomplish when we lean on them exclusively as a means of birthing each moment anew—which is the process of salvation—is the movement of our life experience from one of living in The Kingdom into the bland and inanimate existence of subsisting in The Boredom.

Awakening consciously into the reality of this death experience is definitely not pleasant. For many who enter the path of the heart it comes as a shock. Emotional cleansing is not meant to be pleasurable or easy. It is after all *dying* to the past. Emotional cleansing is a conscious embrace of death while alive. While experiencing it, it may be horrifying, confusing, and seemingly overwhelming on many levels.

However, when we stop running from this deathly shedding of our past—when we stop resisting its shadowy presence as part of life's tide—we invite ourselves to experientially perceive its undeniable consequence: that our life experience is divinely blessed, over and over again, with a rebirth.

By consciously surrendering to the agony of this mental and emotional death experience, we invite the ecstasy of life. Without this consistent shamanic shedding of the skin of time from our psyche, our life has no juice and our eventual physical death no meaning.

Dying daily to the imprinted emotional residue of the past is the Dharma of The Sacred Heart. It is not by banishing death that we re-enter eternal life—it is by fully embracing it.

The Boredom

As we allow ourselves to begin feeling the energetic states we have so long suppressed and sedated—the many feelings that have been an unconscious part of our experience—we gradually reawaken emotional body awareness, together with the vast parameters of felt-perception.

We then begin to real eyes that every aspect of our emotional body that has been consciously or unconsciously suppressed from our awareness numbs our capacity to feel our moment-to-moment life experience.

Fear, anger, and grief are not "things we must get rid of." They are crucial felt-parameters of our emotional body that have been driven into unconsciousness to the point that we have mistaken them for "demons."

By doing everything in our power to exorcise ourselves of these states—to "get rid" of these felt-experiences—we have mistakenly been fanning the fire of a condition that causes us to become numb to life. By mistakenly suppressing our emotional content, we simultaneously suppress *our capacity to feel*.

Without a capacity to feel, *the full vibrancy of the life in which we are always immersed is unfelt by us.*

From the point of *view* of the heart, we are perceptually blinded to the presence of The Kingdom all around us in the world, and so begin looking for The Kingdom somewhere else and in some other time. We no longer resonate with the *feeling of being alive*. Consequently, The Kingdom of Life is veiled in numbness and appears to us as lifeless boredom.

Because we cannot feel the extraordinary resonance of the vibrations of life saturating each moment, we seek out exaggerated and extraordinary experiences as compensation. We begin "seeking God" in strange ways and places, following strange spiritual paths and embracing all sorts of inauthentic behaviors as a desperate attempt to *feel something real*.

The Guardian

WHEN we have diminished emotional body awareness, there is no "doing," no place to go, and no conceptual understanding that leads us back from the experience of boredom and into The Kingdom of Life.

While we remain within this unrealized state of numbness, we unconsciously enter countless mental and physical pathways that invariably lead nowhere.

It is only our reentry into the resonance of *feeling* that transforms this predicament. The capacity to feel enables us to move beyond the bland numbness of an empty life into the juicy fullness of living.

The fullness of the capacity to feel awaits us disguised as a seemingly sleeping three-headed beast—as the serpent of our suppressed fear, anger, and grief. Yet, this serpent is not a beast at all. It is the portal into our hidden inner beauty.

This three-headed dragon guards the gate to The Kingdom of Life and denies entry to all who are too weak of heart to consciously embrace Truth.

‹ 14 ›

Entering the
Vibrational Conversation

THERE is a conversation we are all seeking to consciously participate in—the conversation with the vibrational.

Some call this conversation "the spiritual experience" or "self-
realization" or "God-realization." Throughout this text, we have re-
ferred to it as a conversation with the unspeakable. Yet, we may also call
it a conversation with the *vibrational*.

In this day and age, the word vibrational is more accessible than the
word spiritual, because the word vibrational has no emotional charge
and is not weighed down by superstitious and religious indoctrination.
The word vibrational also holds within it a clue as to how we enter this
conversation.

The vibrational resonance of whatever God is for us is so gentle,
subtle, and fine that—in our mundane, physically trance fixed condition—it appears as silence, stillness, and invisibility. Yet, it is a
vibration that may be experientially perceived by any human being
because it is our birthright to experience it. Indeed, to engage consciously
in this conversation is why we are here.

Initially, this vibrational resonance is too subtle to be encountered
by our physical body. Although we *are it,* and are constantly *within
it,* we cannot perceive it with our physical eyes, hear it with our physical ears, or touch it with our physical flesh. These perceptual abilities
are too dense and impotent in frequency capacity.

Neither can we encounter this vibration experientially through our
thoughts, concepts, or ideas. A thought form does not have a capacity
to experientially encounter a vibration. It can only "think" about it.

The reality of the existence of this vibrational realm is therefore initially not accessible to the physical and mental and emotional bodies, and if these are the only means by which we attempt to approach it, we fail.

This failure is the root of why we end up embracing weird physical practices and resorting to wild mental constructs and imaginings. When we only approach what God is for us through the mental and physical, we invariably end up using fabrication as a means to compensate for our failed attempts. When we perform strange physical practices and use our imagination in an attempt to directly encounter what God is for us, we are lost.

It is not necessary to imagine what is real.

Initially, the vibrational resonance of whatever God is for us—which *is* also us—is encountered through felt-perception. Only the heart has the capacity, the vocabulary, and the perceptual frequency capable of experientially entering this reality.

The Heart Is a Door

OUR physical, mental, and emotional bodies have very different capacities as far as communication is concerned.

If we were to give everyone on the planet the same cup of water and ask them to weigh the cup, and then to measure the quantity of water, all would arrive at the same answers. This is because the physical aspect of our experience is extremely limited. This is why it is such an uncomfortably stifling experience for us when we are physically trance fixed by our experience.

If we were to give everyone on the planet the same cup of water and ask them to write a one-page essay about it, there would be many variations in what is written, but also similarities. This is because our mental capacity is somewhat more expanded than the physical, though it still has its limitations. The ability for us to express ourselves mentally is confined by the limited parameters of our language— by our use of words. There are only so many words and concepts attached to "a cup of water." There is only so much we can "spell."

If we were to give everyone on the planet an opportunity to share their emotions about water, here too we would discover a range of different emotions. People who live in a desert are likely to have quite different emotions from those who experienced Hurricane Katrina or the tsunami in the Indian Ocean. These emotions would range from longing to outright fear.

On the other hand, if we were to show everyone on the planet a cup of water and ask them how, in their heart—quite seperate from their conditioned emotional reactions—they *feel* about water, the range of self-perception that is available would be vast. This is because the heart is vast. The subtleties of our heart are so vast that, although this body is not unlimited, it verges on being unlimited.

The heart is virtually unlimited in its capacity to engage varying ranges of feelings because it is the means by which we are to enter our experiential encounter with that which is unlimited. It is the only attribute within the components of the mind-matrix that has the capacity, the vocabulary, that is capable of entering a conversation with the unspeakable. This immense capacity, with its almost unlimited vocabulary, is called felt-perception.

Accordingly, the heart is the doorway to experientially encountering what God is for us. Only the heart has the capacity to be open to—and engage directly and experientially with—the unlimited.

Only by *feeling what God is* do we really *know God is*.

Initially, feeling is the only vocabulary that has the capacity to interact directly and intimately with the vibrational. Until we integrate this realization, we are deprived of direct experience.

The Language of Heaven

ONCE we are able to consciously contain and fully integrate the immensity of our fear, anger, and grief, we make an astounding discovery. We real eyes we each have the exact amount of fear, anger, and grief within our emotional body that, when fully felt, awakens the entire vocabulary of felt-perception required to equip us with the capacity to experientially enter a conversation with the vibrational.

We have struggled with our fear, anger, and grief because we *think* these states are our enemies and that we must therefore get rid of them. Yet, they are not really fear, anger, or grief. These three words are merely conceptual *spells* in which we have framed unconscious energetic patterns that reflect places within our emotional body in which we are experiencing great resistance.

These spelled words (spells) and their psychological connotations (sentences) cause us to run from and attempt to *re-cover* from these emotional states, instead of *dis-covering* and embracing the real treasure inherent within them.

Our fear, anger, and grief, and all the variety of uncomfortable emotional states emanating from within this trinity of energetic dysfunction, are the as-yet unrealized letters of the alphabet of felt-perception through which, once they are consciously integrated, we commune with the vibrational.

As long as we suppress and sedate these emotional states, wesimultaneously suppress and sedate the various letters of this felt-alphabet— the a-b-c of our ability to speak with what God is for us.

Running from Heaven

IT is no wonder we feel as if nothing is happening and consequently engage in all manner of physical and mental activity in vain attempts to have an experiential encounter with the "spiritual."

It is no wonder we meditate for years and years and feel as if we accomplish nothing, and end up having to fabricate experiences in order to convince ourselves we are having some sort of spiritual encounter.

It is no wonder individuals who call themselves by fancy spiritual names and who adorn themselves in impressive spiritual clothing are able to pull the wool over our eyes and lead us astray.

If we cannot *feel,* we do not know what is *real.*

If we cannot feel, then it matters not that we live in heaven. Our life is still hellishly boring! By in any way running from our fear, anger, and grief, we are running from the experience of "heaven on earth."

The Tool of Appreciation

IF a parent gives their teenager a sum of money, and the teenager reacts to this offering by saying, "I don't want this, I want something else," the parent still takes care of the teenager in many other ways—as long as the teenager's reactive behavior does not resist these experiences as well. However, the parent does not give the teenager any more money, because this gift is not *appreciated*.

Appreciation is a word that has a dual meaning. If we appreciate something, it means we are grateful for it. We acknowledge it accordingly. On the other hand, if we own and trade stocks and shares, and they appreciate, it means they increase in value—they become more.

Appreciation is therefore a creative technology. As a word, it is imbedded with the letters that spell "creation." Appreciation is the act of increasing through gratitude.

Usually we associate a positive emotional signature with the word appreciation. Yet its resonance as a creative tool is neutral.

Whatever we place our attention upon becomes more *because* we place our attention upon it. If we talk about terror, read about terror, think about terror, watch fear-based programming on the television, then *we appreciate terror*. This is why all masters of manifestation instruct us to place our attention on the feelings of what we seek, not upon what we do not seek.

What the Child Appreciates

OUR life as it is right now is a crystal clear reflection of what we most appreciate. What we have most of right now is what we place most of our attention on.

This may not be obvious to us right now because, when we have little to no emotional body awareness, we do not real eyes it is our child self—the condition of our emotional body—that unconsciously drives the focus of our attention.

Until we consciously enter and integrate the condition of our emotional body, this imprinted energetic pattern drives the focus of what we appreciate on our behalf. It directs our appreciation into what it believes will satisfy our unintegrated needs and wants.

Until we consciously enter our emotional body and alert ourselves to its authentic condition, which in turn reveals to us why our life experience is manifesting the way it is, it appears as if life is consistently giving us what we do not want.

This lack of awareness of the authentic condition of our emotional body is why it appears as if life is "happening to us." The moment we become acquainted with the authentic condition of our emotional body, we real eyes our life experience is always an outer manifestation of the unintegrated condition of our emotional body—that our unfolding life experience is an unconscious attempt to compensate for our emotions of fear, anger, and grief.

It is only when we consciously take charge of the condition of our emotional body, and witness the consequences of this level of personal responsibility, that we real eyes our life is an ongoing outer radiance of our inner energetic condition.

Once we connect the dots of the inner and the outer, we stand upon the threshold of divine alchemy.

Stop Running

IF a parent gives their teenager a sum of money, and the money is increased, the parent gives the teenager more money because they know the gift is appreciated. In fact, because the child appreciates what it is given, the parent, realizing that what is given is appreciated, one day gives the child everything.

When we, in any way, push our current life experience away, we are rejecting what is given. We are demonstrating that we are incapable of appreciating it.

When we stop running from our fear, anger, and grief—and its manifestation of confusion within our mental processes, and pain and discomfort within our physical experience—our relationship with what life is undergoes a transformation. This transformation is only possible when we cease reacting to the condition of our emotional body and instead start responding to it—in other words, when we start appreciating it as it is.

This response—a resonance of appreciation—is only possible when we begin to real eyes that the unintegrated condition of our emotional body is the source of the vocabulary of the felt-perception of the heart that we require to enter a conversation with the vibrational.

Once we truly real eyes this, we automatically diminish our reactive reflex to sedate, control, cut out, numb, and drug our felt experiences.

Only then are we able to integrate the realization that *everything within our physical, mental, and emotional experience that is unfamiliar or uncomfortable is actually what God is for us, winking at us in a language we cannot yet speak.*

To awaken fully to this language, and to be able to converse fluently in it, requires feeling what is happening to us in each moment without judgment, agenda, or concern—and without attempting to stop these feelings or change them into something else.

This transformation in our perceptual relationship with the felt aspect of our life experience enables us to stop running from this moment and instead begin settling into it. One of the automatic consequences of allowing ourselves to settle into the moment is that we experience a gradual decline in addictive and inauthentic behavior.

It is only at this point in our journey that we become vulnerable to an ascended definition of what the resonance of "joy" really is.

‹ 15 ›

The Pursuit of Happiness

I N life, we are either *in charge* or *driven by a charge*.

Being *in charge* is only possible when we take responsibility for the causal point of the quality of our experience and all the parameters of our outer behavior by interacting with our life through felt perception.

Carrying a charge is when we are driven unconsciously into behaviors of sedation and control by the uncomfortable, unintegrated condition of our emotional body—by the unhappy child.

When we are driven by a charge, we enter an endless and desperate state of *doing*, also called "the pursuit of happiness." The pursuit of happiness is a belief that the quality of our experience is determined by physical events and circumstances. It is the belief that something must *happen* for us to feel good.

When we are physically trance fixed by our experience, happiness is "a happening." Not only must something specific *happen*, but something specifically must also *not happen*—namely, those events and circumstances we believe are the cause of our unhappiness.

When we are involved in the pursuit of happiness, we are actively trying to make certain things happen—and once we get them to happen, attempting to keep them happening. Simultaneously, we are actively trying to stop other events and circumstances from happening—and *if* we accomplish this, attempting to keep them from ever happening.

That which we seek to happen becomes "good," and that which we seek to keep from happening becomes "bad."

"Good" then becomes our god, and "bad" our devil.

Because we do not have emotional body awareness, we cannot perceive that the pursuit of happiness is an outwardly projected energetic war that is actually taking place *within our own emotional body*.

Our outer behavior is a reflection of us inwardly running towards emotions we are familiar with and away from those that appear alien. This internal division is then reflected within our mental body as confusion, and outwardly in our life experience as ongoing chaos and conflict in our physical circumstances.

What we do not real eyes as we desperately battle to keep certain circumstances happening—and to keep others *from* happening—is that the only constant of our physical experience is that it is constantly changing. Consequently, trying to make something happen, and then to keep it happening, is impossible, and only serves to make us desperately unhappy.

In other words, *the pursuit of happiness is the source of our unhappiness*.

Joy Is Not An Emotion

WHEN we are involved in the pursuit of happiness, we assume that joy is an emotion. We imagine that joy is a state other than what we are currently experiencing—a state in which we feel exceedingly happy all the time. This is a major perceptual error.

Joy may be expressed physically, mentally, and emotionally, but it is not an emotion. *Joy is a relationship we have with our emotional body.*

Joy is a relationship we have with our emotional body in which we allow ourselves to feel *all* emotions, whether they are pleasing or not, comfortable or not, familiar or not.

We allow ourselves to feel all emotional states moving through our field of experience because we embrace the vast array of feelings within these emotional states—*especially* those that are uncomfortable and unfamiliar—as the letters of a felt-alphabet that empowers us to consciously commune with the vibrational.

In other words, we may awaken one morning feeling an emotional resonance that in the past we may have described as feeling depressed. Instead of reacting negatively to this experience by canceling our activities, altering our schedule, or moaning to others in an attempt to get their attention, we choose to observe our state with awareness. We do not attempt to adjust our experience with pharmaceuticals or through any physical behavior. We do not allow ourselves to start telling a story about what we *think* is happening to us. We do not behave as if something is wrong, or as if this should not be happening. Instead, we allow our attention to rest compassionately upon this strangely uncomfortable energetic resonance as we move throughout our day. Consequently, when our day comes to a close, we real eyes we have experienced our life more deeply. We have *felt* something.

This is of course not easy. But as we enter heart-work, we real eyes that "easy" is overrated. Joy is not about feeling good or having life be easy. Joy is about *feeling everything* and having life *be just as it is*.

As long as we are still navigating our experiences towards that which is easy, we automatically navigate away from that which makes life real. This is why we enter *the boredom*.

Joy takes us beyond boredom into The Kingdom of Life, where all is constantly created anew through *the embrace of the unknown*. The pursuit of happiness, on the other hand, is a constant stance of *avoid-dance*—a dance *around the void* instead of *into* it.

Beyond Polarity

WHILE upon Earth, one of the realities we encounter is duality. The tides of our human experience are constantly fluctuating between day and night, hot and cold, hard and soft, up and down, light and dark, in and out, young and old, strong and weak, and so on.

These seemingly opposing states initiate and support the experience of movement, change, differentiation, growth, and transformation. The flow of these polar opposites is healthy, natural, and, when perceived through integrated awareness, awesome in its seemingly unending and ever-blending beauty.

Whenever we consciously or unconsciously initiate behaviors in an attempt to control or sedate what is happening to us in the moment—behaviors that deny *what is* and instead try to pull into being *what is not*—we automatically enter a segregation consciousness that feeds off the natural tendency for polar opposites here on Earth.

If we try to feel better, we end up feeling worse. If we try to make things easier, we end up making them harder. If we try to enforce peace, we seed conflict. If we try to be good, we become evil. Hence those wise expressions of warning like "more haste, less speed."

The profound nature of the present moment is that it has no opposite.

The present moment, when entered and embraced exactly as it is, is always unique because it is always reborn anew. Each moment has never happened before and so cannot be compared to any other. Being unique, it has no polar opposite.

Entering the present moment delivers us beyond the realm of opposites even when we are constantly embraced within the unending tidal experience of seemingly opposing circumstances. It is a fertile portal for conscious entry into a non-polar paradigm. This is the miracle of entering the present moment and embracing it unconditionally.

The Straight and Narrow

MANY have contemplated the instruction that we are to "walk the straight and narrow." But what does this mean?

When emotionally, mentally, or physically approached, this profound instruction inevitably leads to not allowing ourselves to feel certain emotions, practicing enforced mental rules, and engaging in dictatorial self-supressing behaviors. Because of the ever-present potential of polarities here upon Earth, predetermined rules and behaviors imposed mindlessly upon the uniquely reborn circumstances of the moment simultaneously seed the opposite of what they intend.

To force any moment to inauthentically produce the fruit of pleasure is to plant a crop of pain.

Subsequently, no matter how well intended, a mental and physical approach to walking the straight and narrow becomes an unintended nest for self-destructive, self-defeating, and self-sabotaging behavior. This is what is meant by "the road to hell—separation consciousness—is paved with good intentions."

However, when we enter an unconditional relationship with our heart as a means of embracing the moment just as it is, we awaken into a consistently rebirthing encounter with life that is beyond the tide of polarities. We experientially embrace what is conceptually called "oneness." This honoring of the moment, just as it is, by feeling it as fully as possible, is "to walk the straight and narrow."

Only the texture of the present, and our unconditional honoring of it, truly unveils what it means to traverse this human experience in a holistic and hence holy manner. This is the profound revelation awaiting us within the fabric of each moment.

This Is It

WHEN we stop running from that which we perceive as uncomfortable and unfamiliar, and instead embrace it, we gradually reawaken an awareness of our heart. This enables us to begin feeling everything more deeply.

Instead of fleeing what is, we start settling into the moment we are always in—*no matter what*.

We feel the unlimited variations of the radiance of our own presence, and we consciously appreciate this. We feel the unlimited radiance of the presence of others, and we consciously appreciate this. We feel the ever-changing and unlimited currents of energy swirling through every day, and we consciously appreciate this. We feel the presence of nature in all her manifestations, and we consciously appreciate this.

Not surprisingly, the more we consciously appreciate what we allow ourselves to feel, the deeper our capacity to feel becomes.

As we allow this experience of felt-perception to unfold, a remarkable discovery dawns within our awareness like a rising sun after a long dark night:

THIS LIFE, THE ONE THAT WE ARE LIVING RIGHT NOW, JUST AS IT IS IN EACH MOMENT, IS "THE SPIRITUAL EXPERIENCE" WE HAVE BEEN SEEKING.

Awakening Into the Journey

WE are unable to real eyes that the experience we are having right now is the destination of our heart's quest because, by suppressing our emotional body awareness, we are unable to *feel it to be so*. The more deeply we allow ourselves to feel, the more obvious this realization becomes.

As this realization dawns within our awareness, we automatically begin embracing our life experience just as it is right now with deeper and deeper appreciation. This deepening appreciation is like the teenager taking the money from the parent and increasing it through acknowledgement and gratitude.

Because we deepen our appreciation of our life experience, this profound gift of our entire encounter with what life is deepens, and deepens, and deepens—eternally.

It is through this portal of continual, eternal deepening of the resonance of our life experience through felt-perception that we enter another realization:

BECAUSE WHATEVER GOD IS FOR US IS INFINITE, THE JOURNEY INTO SELF AND GOD-REALIZATION IS ETERNAL.

There is no "point of arrival."

The result of this realization is that we let go of destination-consciousness and instead embrace journey-consciousness. Our destination becomes experiencing the fullness of the journey of life in the moment it is unfolding.

The Enlightenment Trap

ONE of the most powerful realizations we uncover when we turn inward and embrace our emotional body as the causal point of the quality of our experience is this:

THE QUEST FOR "ENLIGHTENMENT" IS A MENTALLY-DRIVEN PERCEPTUAL DISTRACTION.

The quest for enlightenment leads us to believe there is a state of being outside the one we are experiencing right now that can in some way liberate us from the discomfort of our current experience. It leads us to believe there is a destination, a point of arrival, that once attained is the answer to all our unhappiness.

Enlightenment, just like many "spiritual paths," is the wolf called "the pursuit of happiness" wearing sheep's clothing.

Through embracing the fullness of our moment-to-moment feelings, whether they are familiar to us or not, we awaken to the realization that the heart is the means and the portal through which we commune authentically with our vibrational essence.

By consciously interacting with our life experience through felt-perception, we are able to peer more deeply into the timeless face of what life truly is, and so into our own authentic identity.

This is when we real eyes that it is not some state outside our current experience that we have been seeking. Our authentic quest is to *become increasingly intimate with this experience*—the one we are already in.

This is when we real eyes it is *intimacy* that we seek, not enlightenment.

"Enlightenment" is a mental concept that involves entering physical and mental practices geared towards us attaining an experience that was had by someone else. It is a conceptual trap that intentionally and unintentionally robs us of entering the consequences of appreciating what is given to us right now, in each moment—our current life experience in all its wondrous and often unfathomable beauty.

To appreciate the magnificence of our experience, in this moment, no matter what expression life's face shows us, is to *be* enlightened.

Intimacy

THE possibility of experiencing intimacy may be communicated mentally, and the experience of intimacy may be expressed physically, but to enter into intimacy fully requires reawakening our emotional body awareness.

Intimacy, to be known, is a felt-encounter.

Intimacy is a perceptual embrace in which our felt-perception unwraps *all* our experiences as a means to see more deeply into ourselves—*into-me-and-see*. To enter intimacy, we open the eyes of the heart and use these as the causal point of our perceptual relationship within our physical, mental, and emotional life experience.

Intimacy is *the heart of the matter*.

Once we awaken to the resonance of intimacy through the reawakening of emotional body awareness, we declare, "I once was blind, but now I see."

To experience intimacy, we leave the experience of "the kitchen" and return to our seat within the restaurant of life. We now know about the intimate workings of the kitchen and are proficient as chefs, but we do not live within the confines of the kitchen. Instead, we re-enter life on life's terms and feel blessed by every opportunity to share the food, company, and ever-changing conversation we experience through our human encounter.

Heart Response

ONCE we leave the experience of "the kitchen" and re-enter the dining area, we may appear to others as ordinary and normal human beings. Yet, we are not; we have transformed the normal into the ever-changing, and the ordinary into a constantly unexpected, unfolding miracle.

We now move through our life experience without attempting to manufacture attention through drama. When we encounter any emotional, mental, or physical turbulence along the winding pathways of our eternal journey, we do not react outwardly—we respond inwardly.

Our response is to allow what is happening, feel it as deeply as possible, and embrace these feelings as a wink in the vocabulary of God that is as yet unspeakable to us.

Through feeling the unfamiliar, we constantly awaken to "the great unknown." By feeling deeply, we gradually expand the parameters of our felt-perception, and subsequently deepen our ability to commune intimately with the vibrational resonance inherent in everything.

We do not have to adopt any strange practices, call ourselves by a spiritual name, or enter any behavior that demands inauthentic attention. Our spirituality is not in any thing or activity we do. It is in consciously engaging the invisible felt-resonance running through the entirety of our being.

Our spirituality is in our conscious and consistent response to our heart.

Rest in Peace

THROUGH the fruits of felt-perception, we real eyes it is our soul responsibility to keep our heart open so that we may receive an ongoing and deepening awareness of the peace that is already given.

When we keep our heart open, this peace radiates automatically from the vibrational, through the portal of our heart, into the fabric of our emotions and thought forms, and throughout our physical circumstances. This felt-perception of peace blossoms as effortless joy, abundance, and health.

Because we no longer either defend or attack, to others we may be perceived as meek. But meekness does not mean weakness. On the contrary, it requires becoming a warrior of the heart, and the battle lines are clearly drawn. We do not entertain the illusionary drama of outer opposition. We do not interfere (enter fear) with the experiences of others. We have compassion, but we do not enter sympathy or become concerned. We do not have to "do things just to have fun." We are not bored. By all accounts, to others we may appear as nobody special doing nothing remarkable.

Yet, we wear a quiet inner smile that cannot be bought financially or gained through mental debate. We are sitting in the restaurant, eating our food, and enjoying the dance of life swirling around us. We are in the midst of the same experience as everyone else—we are just responding differently to it. We are taking responsibility for it. We are feeling it as deeply as possible.

Though others may stand next to us and feel as if they are walking through the valley of the shadow of death, we are consciously in the felt-embrace of heaven.

We have discovered why the word "earth" and "heart" are the same, just spelled differently.

We have not fallen for the trap of trying to bring peace to this earth—we have awoken ourselves into the resonance of peace while upon it.

While here, still alive in this awesome physical body, we have consciously entered "heaven on earth."

‹ 16 ›

Parting Fable

ONCE upon a time there was a rabbit and a turtle. One day God appeared before each of them in a dream and said: "I have an important task for you. I want you to travel to a certain place." In the dream God showed them the place. Then God added, "When you get there, I will personally come and meet you."

Rabbit and turtle, inspired by their dreams, set off immediately as instructed.

Rabbit did not waste any time at all and ran straight there.

Turtle set off too, but moments after starting noticed a butterfly drinking from a dewdrop in the gorgeous early morning light of the new day. So, turtle stopped to watch.

Then turtle set off again, but after a few moments noticed a leaf dancing on the water to the rhythm of the morning breeze. So, turtle stopped to watch.

This went on and on and on, and therefore it took turtle almost an eternity to reach the instructed destination.

When God showed up, God asked rabbit: "So rabbit, what did you see?"

"Actually," said rabbit, "I really didn't see anything; I came straight here to see you."

"Oh," said God with a smile. "That was diligent of you."

Then God turned to turtle and asked, "What did you see, turtle?"

"Well," said turtle. "As I was leaving, I noticed a butterfly drinking from a dewdrop in the gorgeous early morning light of the new day." He then told God all about it in the most deliberate detail.

"Then," turtle continued, "as I was about to continue on my way, I noticed a leaf dancing on the water to the rhythm of the morning breeze." He again told God all about it in the most deliberate detail.

There was so much to tell about his journey that it took turtle an eternity to describe each detail of the journey. Consequently, God spent eternity with turtle.

Don't be a silly rabbit.

Epilogue: To Be Continued

DURING the writing of *Alchemy of the Heart*, I experienced a deepening in my understanding of what the heart is.

My insight is that the portal between the vibrational—the inner realm—and the emotional, mental, and physical—the outer expression of this inner realm—is *the feeling body*. This feeling body is what we metaphorically refer to as *the heart*. The heart is therefore an intermediary, a hinge and a portal, between the vibrational and its expression within the emotional, mental, and physical.

The heart and the emotional body are therefore not the same.

The heart has the capacity to interact inwardly with the vibrational and, simultaneously, outwardly with and through the emotional, mental, and physical.

Whenever we experience a realization through in-sight, mystical revelation, and creative inspiration, we are witnessing the perceptual capacity of the heart to absorb emanations from within the vibrational, and then to communicate these into our human world through the emotional, mental, and physical. Our heart therefore oversees our capacity to draw from within and express what is accessed outwardly.

As long as our emotional body is unintegrated, our awareness of our heart as this hinge or portal into the vibrational remains obscured.

Being emotional does not therefore imply that we are functioning from our heart—or that we are even aware of our heart. It implies we are being driven unconsciously by the unintegrated condition of our current emotional content—by our fear, anger, and grief.

This insight empowers us to differentiate between *feeling* and *emotion*.

Feeling is the perceptual capacity of our heart. *Emotions* are an energetic expression of the vibrational into creation—expressions of varying conditions of energy in motion, or not in motion—that our heart is able to perceive through its feeling capacity.

Just as the heart may feel varying energetic conditions within the emotional body, so too is it able to feel the quality of the thoughts within the mental body, and the variety of sensations within our physical circumstances. The bottom line is that it's the heart that feels.

The next book in this series will explore our journey into fully awakening the capacities of our heart—our felt-perception—through the experience of intimacy. Intimacy invites *the intent to real eyes what love is beyond all programmed definitions and conditions.*

It's through intimacy that we fully awaken the feeling capacity of the heart, enabling us to perceive what love is. The awakening of this capacity completes our healing journey so we may consciously embrace our inheritance as co-creators within the eternal country of consciousness.

Once we have awoken our capacity, through felt-perception, to authentically contain the immensity of what love is, we are simultaneously endowed with the vulnerability that invites a direct encounter with whatever God is for us.

This wonderful exploration into and through intimacy as a means to plunge heart-first into the vibrational is a conversation I look forward to sharing with you.

Kind regards,
Michael

The Presence Process
MICHAEL BROWN

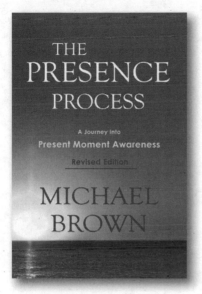

Why is it so difficult to simply be present? The reason is that our deeply suppressed emotional imprints from childhood distract us from an awareness of the present moment. Until this "emotional charge" from our past is integrated, all our attempts to quiet our thoughts and access the peace, joy, and love that are bedrock to our being are of only limited success.

We all long to be free of discomfort and experience inner peace. However, the attempt to get rid of our discomfort is misguided. As South African Michael Brown explains in his revised book, *The Presence Process - A Journey Into Present Moment Awareness*, we aren't broken and don't need to be "healed." Rather, our discomfort needs to be integrated, so that the trapped energy of reactive emotion becomes available to empower us in everyday life.

The Presence Process itself is a journey that guides us into taking responsibility for our emotional integration. It's a way to consciously "grow up," which enables us to live consciously in the present moment, taking charge of every aspect of our experience.

The Presence Process teaches us how to exercise authentic personal responsibility in a practical manner. It offers a simple, practical approach to experiencing personal peace in the midst of globally accelerating change, discomfort, conflict, and chaos.

When you embark on The Presence Process you will be joining thousands of others who have taken this powerful ten week journey to peace, joy, love, and a new sense of personal empowerment. The revised edition of *The Presence Process - A Journey Into Present Moment Awareness* is available at Namaste Publishing's website.

www.namastepublishing.com

namaste
PUBLISHING

books that change your life

Our Service Territory Expands

Since introducing Eckhart Tolle to the world with *The Power of Now* in 1997 (and later with *Stillness Speaks*, *A New Earth*, and *Milton's Secret*), NAMASTE PUBLISHING has been committed to bringing forward only the most evolutionary and transformational publications that acknowledge and encourage us to awaken to who we truly are: spiritual beings of inestimable value and creative power.

In our commitment to expand our service purpose—indeed, to redefine it—we have created a new website like no other. We are creating a global spiritual gathering place to support and nurture ongoing individual and collective evolution in consciousness.

As a member of the Namaste Spiritual Community online, you will have access to our publications in a variety of formats, plus supporting resources found exclusively on our site. The discussion groups will center around a variety of topics including spirituality, health, and relationships, as well as our most popular titles. You will have access to Namaste authors through their blogs, discussion forums, and a myriad of multimedia content. And because we are all teachers and learners, you will have the opportunity to meet other members and share your thoughts, update and share your "spiritual status," and contribute to our interactive online spiritual dictionary.

Here you will also find the wisdom of Bizah, a loveable student of Truth, dished up in daily and weekly doses. You will also find rich content from our authors' and publisher's blogs, as well as timely guidance found in our daily Compassionate Eye blog.

What better way to come to experience the reality and benefits of our Oneness than by gathering in spiritual community? Tap into the exponential power to create a more conscious and loving world when two or more gather with this same noble intention.

We request the honor of your presence at
www.namastepublishing.com